This Zine Book Belongs to

Aaron Garoutte

the book of

zines

Readings from the Fringe

edited by

Chip Rowe

an owl book
henry holt and company
new york

Henry Holt and Company, Inc.
Publishers since 1866
115 West 18th Street
New York, New York 10011

Henry Holt® is a registered trademark
of Henry Holt and Company, Inc.

Published in Canada by Fitzhenry & Whiteside Ltd.,
195 Allstate Parkway, Markham, Ontario L3R 4T8.

Library of Congress Cataloging-in-Publication Data
The book of zines: readings from the fringe / edited by
Chip Rowe—1st Owl ed.
p.   cm.
Includes index. "An Owl Book."
I. Rowe, Chip.
AC5.B58   1997
081—dc21   97-453
                           CIP

Alternative Cataloging-in-Publication Data
Rowe, Chip, editor.
The book of zines: readings from the fringe. New York: H. Holt, 1997.
Illustrated with black-and-white photos, comic strips, and cartoons.

Includes excerpts from *Beer Frame, bOING bOING, Bust, Chip's Closet Cleaner,
Cometbus, Hitch, Meanwhile . . . , Mystery Date, Nancy's Magazine, Pathetic Life,
Pawholes,* and others, as well as index.

PARTIAL CONTENTS: Advice.—Chow.—Computers.—Conspiracies.—Dating—
Deviants.—Drugs.—Fame.—Fashion.—Games.—Jokers.—Kooks.—Lists.—Movies.—
Pests.—Porn.—Rock & roll.—Romance.—Secrets.—Sex ed.—Sports.—Stunts.—
Surveys.—Thrift.—Travel.—Violence.—Work.—How to order a zine.

1. Zines—Excerpts. 2. Popular culture. 3. United States—Social life and
customs. I. Title: The zines book. II: Title: The zine book. III. Title:
Readings from the fringe. IV: Title: Fringe readings.

306 or 818.54 or 973.929—dc21

ISBN 0-8050-5083-3

Henry Holt books are available for special promotions and premiums.
For details contact: Director, Special Markets.

First Owl Edition—1997

Designed by Paula R. Szafranski

Printed in the United States of America
All first editions are printed on acid-free paper. ∞

10 9 8 7 6 5 4 3 2 1

contents

introduction

Whatcha Mean What's a Zine?

Most zines suck. There's no nice way to say it. The truism coined by Theodore Sturgeon applies: Ninety percent of everything is crap. Most people forget what Sturgeon said about the remaining 10 percent. He said it was worth dying for.

I'm dying! Zines (pronounced "zeens," from fanzines) are cut-and-paste, "sorry this is late," self-published magazines reproduced at Kinko's or on the sly at work and distributed through mail order and word of mouth. They touch on sex, music, politics, television, movies, work, food, whatever. They're Tinkertoys for malcontents. They're obsessed with obsession. They're extraordinary and ordinary. They're about strangeness but since it's usually happening somewhere else you're kind of relieved. You can get to know people pretty well through their zines, which are always more personal and idiosyncratic than glossy magazines because glossies and the celebrities they worship are so busy being well known.

Most zine editors can recall the moment they first saw *Factsheet Five*, the zine that reviews zines, and asked themselves (1) *that's* what I've been doing? or, more likely, (2) I can do that, and why not? Everyone cleared space on their kitchen tables, and estimates flew like confetti—ten thousand zines, fifty thousand zines, a million readers. Nobody knows. A zine dies, a zine grows. Over the years since I assembled the first issue of *Chip's Closet Cleaner* and sent copies to my puzzled relatives, I've exchanged zines and letters and e-mail with hundreds of underground publishers and found we share the same desire—the same *need*—to create. *Factsheet Five* used to ask its readers a deceptively simple question, "Why publish?" and always received passionate (if sometimes long-winded) responses.

Zines have a long history. In the early part of this century, they got a kickstart from Dadaists, science fiction fans, anarchists, poets, and other self-starters, along with technology such as the mimeograph. Psychiatrist Fredric Wertham, who discovered zines in the early forties and later wrote a book called *The World of Fanzines*, believed they were "essentially unpolluted by the greed, the arrogance and the hypocrisy that has invaded so much of our intellectual life." He was wrong, of course. Zines were around in the fifties and sixties and then punk rock and its Do-It-Yourself aesthetic pushed them along in the seventies. The arrival of self-service copiers and desktop publishing did the same in the eighties. More recently, zines have become hip. The *Wall Street Journal* gave zines space on its front page while dismissing them as "the bottom of the publishing food chain." The *New York Times* has written about zines three times and declared them "quirky" twice. Some zines now have barcodes and are sold in chain bookstores. Zines have gone online too, for computer savants who crave fancy graphics. Some are good—say about 10 percent.

The method by which you get your hands on a zine has not changed—for best results, send well-wrapped cash and a kind word (addresses for the zines in this collection begin on page 171). You'll get a zine in return; if you don't, the editor needed your money to eat or something. The selections were selected because I liked them—like many zine addicts, I save my favorites in tottering piles. Yet all I did was read. The writers and artists who graciously let me reprint their stuff deserve the kindest words.

Most zines suck, but you find that golden 10 percent and you're hooked for life. Found mine.

— Chip Rowe

a d v i c e

Letter
from
Granpa Vic

*In 1993, Bob Bellerue sent an issue of **BASURA** (now Basurame), his zine devoted to "weird & funky shtuff," to his grandparents. "My parents said it probably wasn't a good idea, but I figured what the heck and sent it off," he recalls. "Within four days I had a letter from my grandfather denouncing the endeavor as trash while also encouraging me to do better. I decided to publish it in issue 3, and as I was laying it out I found out he'd died. I was sad because I couldn't continue the dialogue and somehow make good on his desire to see me as a 'responsible young man.'"*

letter from Granpa Vic   march 30, 93

"Dear Bob:
     Your letter, typed so legibly, gives
me a first clue as to what is going on in
your head. It takes me back to when I was
24 and younger - the worries, the uncer-
tainty, trying to understand the world
and what place I might make for myself.

The 'Basura'-aptly named, a crock of slime.
I will not mince words, Do Not, repeat, B
Do Not,-send such a missive of filth to
your Grandmother. No need to learn that
kind of "literary composition" at Boulder -
anyFlop House toilet or Hobo Jungle can p
provide this type of dirt. There may be
some impressive meassages buried in the
sludge but they are not apparent. The mention concerning John Hinkley could subject
you to federal questioning.   I do
see in certain places a tortured crying
for help and understanding, a searching
for life's meaning - and to this we all
must respond. And you must respond too
with tolerance and patience, and less of
scorn for a world and its conventions,
which have been ages in the developing.
It is easy to ridicule society for its ills
--but what are you doing to set an example?
talk is cheap. Effort and accomplishment
are really and meaningful.
     I did ask you for some product so this
material is considered to be your response.
I have read the letter part with great care
to try and find who you are and how you
see this world. Where are you going?
     After some general comments about
your normal-sounding school you then say
"Iwish I didn't have to be in school." ??
Can you not see the opportunity, the challenge, the chance to develop intellectual-
ly? You are so right when you realize that

if you had nothing to do "work for or with" that you would be Brain-dead. Thats right, that's Life, Life is struggle, solving problems. Life is building your mental and physical muscles to be better able to meet life's challenges and to be proud of your strength and accomplishment. There is no "wish to come true"-there is rather a great big Wonderful World waiting for men of courage and strength - and industry.

That kind of dedication enables your parents to pay your Bills. That kind of effort is necessary so you will be able to provide for your Future Family. This is the real truth about Existence on this Earth.

You are right to see the importance of a "Regular Skilled Job" to provide the basic income to give a good life. And to be able to follow your "Art" independently. But don't overlook the importance of the Basic good job to provide the money that makes the engine run. Your Parents did the necessary, getting hands dirty, to provide for you for 24 years. They faced grubby 10 hour work days, on the road at 6:30 AM and rough and tumble competition to provide for themselves and their children. What have you done with your last 7 years?

Bob, you say you have a "different" world to contend with than we did. That's hog-wash.   Society is not so much becoming Polarized -- as you are missing out on how to play the game.   We had less Drugs in my day but alcoholism was much worse. We had less technology and more hard dirty work. In my day we had the great Depression of 1929, no welfare, no food stamps. You worked - or you would starve! Todays society is a breeze by comparison. But, in any society, whether 1993, 1923, 1850, or 1600 - a man must be able to fund Food and shelter

for his Family and protect them from Danger/.
Todays man must still be strong, smart, and
willing to pay his taxes. Smart talk will
not erase these Basic Facts of Existence.

Bob, I have said this before, But, you
are setting your sights too Low. What you
are espousing is not good enough for you.
My stomach heaves at the thought of you on
the street distributing that "Basura" and
accepting donations. For Christ Sake look
at yourself. Look at where you want to be
in 5 years or 25 years or ? And take the
necessary steps to accomplish your goals.
Be prepared tosweat and strain in a good
cause. Stop your snide attitude toward
routine work, steady wages, and social conventions, and "salivating with Pavlov's
Puppies." You are so afraid of regimenta-
tion - you are in danger of missing the
train of Progress.

Our Forefathers built here the most Wonderful Nation on Earth. It was built by
hard, sweaty work and by honest, thoughtful
Legislation and Rules to live by. Unproduc-
tive Criticism will not change that. But
new ideas and productive Creativity will
make this a better World.

Bob,   that "Basura" helps me to see the
anguished young man searching for the
Meaning fcf Life and his place in it. But
beyond that those disjointed mumbles have
no value/

Your letter, on the other hand, shows a
literate, observant, Friendly human being
who is willing to share a four page acccount
with his Grandparents to let them see a
slice of his life. This letter has worthwhile thoughts which merit dissemination
in the Colorado Papers or magazines. Not
publication just for money but to develop
your power of expression and establish you
as an intellect of value. This should be

your goal - to become an intellectual Force
and not a voice crying in the Wilderness.
Pride yourself on your strength to do a mundane job and eventually attain Financial
independence. And Flex your strong intellect
to accomplish progress, and encourage
Christian Fellowship and economic development!   The World will continue spinning
in spite of all the Criticism gushing forth
--but you must become part of the Solution,
not part of the Problem! Does that make
Sense? Your Grandma and I send our Love
and Prayers for your Future.
                              Granpa

angst

Desperate for Nothing in
Particular for No Particular Reason

In **FUNKAPOTAMUS**, *his zine of cartoons, skateboard-
ing, and enlightenment, Jerome Gaynor offers some
entertaining "tales too true to tell," remembers strange or
frightening dreams, chronicles the daffy adventures of
Otto and Pepe, and recalls the imaginary monsters of his
youth. He recently assembled another great publication,*
Flying Saucer Attack, *in which twenty-five artists depict
the last hours before all human life is destroyed by an
invading force of asshole aliens. This cartoon first
appeared in* funkapotamus 7.

ZINE VOICES

"I love it when I give someone a copy of
my zine and they get excited: 'Is this the
new one!? Rad!'"
                              —Jerome Gaynor, *funkapotamus*

4

baggage

🎭 Janalyzing Eve

Created by siblings Erin and Don Smith in 1989, **TEENAGE GANG DEBS** *is devoted to sitcoms from the late sixties and seventies. That includes, naturally, tons o' material about "The Partridge Family," "My Three Sons," and "The Brady Bunch," including a sit-down with actress Eve Plumb, who played Jan. This excerpt from a much longer interview (they even talked about whatever dinner theater show Eve was in at the time) is one of two Brady Bunch references in this book, but that's it, I swear.*

Erin: What was it like when you were getting the role of Jan Brady? I've heard that they had a brunette set of girls, blond set of boys . . .

Eve Plumb: Right, yeah. So they were mainly choosing by hair color. I was out the first round. So they called me back and looked me over again, and cast me. I never had to read or test or anything.

Erin: How do you feel about the Jan character?

Eve: At that point it wasn't a character. They were pretty much writing a lot of scripts for, you know, our personalities anyway, so I wasn't playing a character. I was just trying to do the lines as best I could.

Don: To me, the Jan character always represented how I felt as a kid. The middle kid (not that I'm a middle child), not the oldest, not the youngest. Riding a bike into the picture, etc.

Eve: I was just doing my job. I didn't have any input. I was just doing what they told me. I was really unaware of a lot of the things that people like to extrapolate from this whole thing. It's, you know . . . it was a TV show.

Erin: Did you save a lot of stuff from the show, like clothes or props?

Eve: No, there was no reason to.

Don: One thing that has always puzzled me is when they put together the beginning intro, did they just tell you to look to your left?

Eve: They had it all timed out, and they shot each of us individually. It was shot without sound so it was one of those funky old noisy cameras on a blue background. They had it all timed out so you looked up five seconds, you looked down, looked left, looked right.

Don: What do you think your favorite episode would be?

Eve: You know, this is so sad, because people ask me all the time, but I don't have one.

Erin: Do people ever call you Jan?

Eve: Occasionally. I just correct them.

FREE ADVICE

"Make friends with 'revolutionary' workers who are in a position to 'comp' your printing bills in the name of 'art.'"

—Greg Beets and Buzz Moran, Hey! Hey! Buffet!

c h o w

 Busting the Buffet

Greg Beets and Buzz Moran's zine, **HEY! HEY! BUFFET!** *serves up generous portions of news and reviews about the grand tradition of stuffing your face. "Nothing illustrates the social kinship of America and the late, great Roman Empire better than the all-you-can-eat*

buffet," they wrote in their first issue after a hearty meal at a place called Casita Flameada. "The Romans called their buffet an orgy and threw in sex and a vomit trough. Hopefully we too will reach this pinnacle someday."

In the interest of preserving the self-indulgent gluttony that keeps America full, we hereby disgorge our 10-step program for busting all-you-can-eat buffets.
Fellow buffeteers, go forth and plunder!

(1) Go to buffets hungry, but not on an empty stomach. Sometimes, when I'm really hungry, I start feeling Lasorda sick. I guess this is God's gift to the terminally famished. A little food keeps your stomach stretched out, which maximizes that great going-into-labor feeling.

(2) Develop a plan of attack. Whether it's salad to entree to dessert or vice versa, remain steadfast to the pattern that will develop as the buffet monkey sinks its claws into your ever-willing flesh.

(3) Do not "hot-dog" through the line on your first trip. It's a buffet, chowderhead! It was there when you walked in and it'll be there when you're full. It's fun to go for seconds!

(4) Always sample a wide array of food. Try a little bit of everything (as long as you're with a consenting adult and there is no violence involved). If the food is hard to swallow, simply push it aside and try something else, got it?

(5) Eat some greens and bread if you can get them. Okay, we're making a little concession to that stupid healthy lifestyle thing. So what? Fiber keeps the digestive freight train rolling solid. That way, all those cancerous food additives don't have time to hook up with a cute enzyme.

(6) Don't eat too much cheese or breaded foods. Overdoing these staples inhibits your ability to down mass quantities of meat—the "money food."

(7) Drink water. For one, it's free. Two, it won't fill you up.

(8) Avoid bender-mixing. Ecchleasyassees tells us there's a time to gorge and a time to imbibe, but commingling such vices casts abomination unto thy guttocks! Maybe you get drunk before eating because it's "cool," or because you think it will enhance your performance. We're sure 17-year-old Burton Dill of Ponder, Texas, thought the same thing when he tried to battle the HomeTown Buffet after drinking two Mickey's Bigmouths. Burton didn't make it to the bathroom.

(9) Don't be ashamed of your gluttony. Women especially should not buy into the media lies designed to turn you into an anorexic waif. Any man worth his bulk will love a woman who holds her own at the trough.

(10) Eat slow. Fast food has bastardized the beautiful art of eating into just another boring bodily function, like sex. Fight back by taking the buffet nice and slow. Make conversation. If you're alone, bring a book or religious tract. Remember, a buffet isn't just a meal, it's a Great Entertainment Value. Don't eat to live—live to eat!

Armour Pork Brains in Milk Gravy

Paul Lukas isn't interested in the hippest, hottest, or latest. He wants ordinary, and he discovers it everywhere in the nooks and crannies of consumer culture. Overlooked products found at the supermarket or shared by friends are carefully examined, tested, and reviewed in **BEER FRAME: The Journal of Inconspicuous Consumption**. *One of his favorite everyday artifacts is the Brannock Device, the chrome contraption shoe stores use to measure your feet (Paul wears a 9D). Other items, such as canned sauerkraut juice, are more mysterious in their appeal. Apparently, it's a killer laxative—and probably goes quite well with pork brains.*

Let's face it, the pork industry has some serious image problems. You've got politicians denouncing every piece of spending legislation they don't like as "full of pork." You've got most of the general populace running around under the mistaken impression that pigs are filthy animals when in fact they're quite clean. And let's not even get started on "Babe."

The people at the National Pork Producers Council recently responded to these problems by running promotional spots during the 1996 Super Bowl. Unfortunately, the bland slogan they unveiled for the occasion—"Pork: Taste What's Next"—makes you wonder if the beef lobby planted a mole amidst the pork bigwigs. Moreover, the commercials neglected to mention pork brains, definitely the sort of product that could use advertising support. Imagine the possibilities: "Pork Brains: The Gray Matter from the Other White Meat."

The very notion of pork brains may sound a bit beyond the pale, but they're a fairly common sight in the canned-goods aisles of the South. Of course, they're a bit harder to come by 'round these parts, which is why I was so pleased when my friend Marie brought back two cans of Armour Pork Brains after visiting her family in Virginia.

The Armour Pork Brains package design, dominated by a photo of a brains-related dish, is unremarkable. A peek at the nutritional information, however, reveals the interesting factoid that a single serving of pork brains provides *1170 percent* of our recommended daily cholesterol intake. All the more brilliant, then, that the label includes a recipe for "Scrambled Eggs and Brains," which sounds like the kind of meal that keeps bypass surgeons in business. The recipe leads off with instructions to "Drain brains"—I bet someone at Armour is still chuckling over that one.

Curious to learn more about the culinary applications of pork brains, I called the Armour consumer-response line (where a recording helpfully reminded me that the firm's product line also

includes Armour Ground & Formed Sliced Dried Beef, one of those product names that has way too many adjectives for its own good). Sadly, the only recipe they had on file was for the afore-mentioned eggs 'n' brains. Operating under the theory that almost anything tastes good fried, I tossed some brains into a hot skillet with oil, cooked them until they seemed done (a rather subjective notion, admittedly), and tentatively brought a forkful to my mouth. A few moments later my cats were enjoying the rest of the brains and I was working on a new theory.

In short, brains taste nasty. All of which brings up a question of dinner-party etiquette: Just what does one do when offered a plate of steaming pork brains by a well-meaning but sadly misguided host? I'm sure Emily Post never covered this one, but Armour has conveniently provided an excuse. The brains are canned in milk gravy, providing squeamish diners the perfect opportunity to graciously say, "Oh, *brains!* You know, I really love them, but unfortunately I'm lactose intolerant. Could you pass the biscuits?" By interesting coincidence, Marie—the one who procured the brains for me in the first place—is lactose intolerant herself. Or so she claims. (The Dial Corp., Food Division, 15101 North Scottsdale Dr., Scottsdale, AZ 85077; 800-528-0849)

Stay Free!
Alive with pleasure!

$2.95

It's a Doughboy!

In 1992, Carrie McLaren was a college rep for Sony Music. On a whim, she started a zine called Sonyland. *It was well received, but the moment Carrie realized what she was doing (an "underground" publication for a huge international corporation), she bolted. Joining forces with local bands Spatula and Evil Weiner, she cleared her conscience by revving up* **STAY FREE!** *This interview with the Pillsbury Doughboy, conducted by Carrie and Jason Torchinsky at a North Carolina supermarket, appeared in issue 10. "The original plan was for two* *of my friends to take off their clothes in the store so we could snap photos of the Doughboy in action with this naked couple," Carrie says. "Unfortunately, they chickened out."*

On October 29, the Pillsbury Doughboy visited our very own Carrboro. For three hours, he pressed the dough and signed autographs, always wearing a smile. As we discovered, getting a Doughboy's attention isn't easy. So we asked a Pillsbury sales rep for some background.

What's it like to work with the Doughboy?
Sales Rep: We set up this special time to interact with the public, hand out coupons, display product. And the kids get to meet the Doughboy.

Does the Doughboy ever have to leave the store?
The Doughboy also goes to malls, parades, and things like that, if that's what you mean.

What's his standard day like? Does he have a desk he sits at?
[long pause] He pretty much works on overseeing people making product, going out and making sure people are buying.

So he's an expediter. Kinda like quality control.
[changing subject] Kids love him.

How long does it take him to get ready?
About 15 minutes.

Really?! To put on the hat, I guess. Does he go through any warm-up exercises or anything?
No.

He's a natural!

[Another sales rep walks up. The first one suggests we talk to her, then walks off. We exchange hellos.]

We just want to know what it's like working with a legend in the packaged food industry.
Sales Rep 2: We travel—I have seventy-two grocery stores—we travel to sale promotions such as this. It gets the customers involved and creates a lot of excitement.

I noticed it says on the flyers the Doughboy is eight feet tall. Do you think there'd be much difference between, say, a six-foot Doughboy and . . .
Again, it creates excitement, people are wondering: What's going on here? Is there a person inside?

[Sales Rep 2 starts asking us questions about what publication we work for. The supermarket manager comes over with the first sales rep and they try to kick us out. We drop the regional manager's name and they go away. The Doughboy walks up, smiling.]

What brings you to Carrboro?
Doughboy: Didn't the sales reps answer your questions?

We want to hear from you!
I heard Carolina was playing State today.

You're a big basketball fan, eh?
No, football fan.

Oh. Well, let me ask you: You're made of dough and the products you sell are made of dough. Do you have any problem with that?
[no reply]

That doesn't bother you? You're secure with that?
Well, I've got to do my job.

Do you get a lot of fat jokes from people?
Sometimes, but it's okay.

How did you start in this? How did you become a Doughboy?
[long pause, seems nervous] Um, I don't know. I was born into it.

What sort of privileges do you have as a Doughboy? Does it carry a lot of clout?
I'm not really interested in the celebrity thing.

You looking for that special Doughgirl?
There already is one—Poppin' Fresh.

So do you get to hang out much with other fictional characters?
Sometimes.

The Keebler guys?
Yeah, well, they're a little small and they get underfoot, but Ernie's okay.

Weren't you rapping in a commercial a couple years ago? What was the inspiration for that?
That was a point of contention so what happened was . . . well, it wasn't really me.

You were lip synching?
Pretty much.

Has there ever been anything else they wanted you to do in a commercial that you thought wasn't Doughboy-style?
They wanted me to do a nude scene once, you know, take off my hat, so I walked.

Are you of any relation to the Doughboys of WWI?
No.

Where do you see yourself in ten years?
Well, I'd like to direct.

[Small child walks up and asks if the Doughboy can see. Of course he can see!]

What are you going to be for Halloween?
The Sta-Puff Marshmallow Man.

Wow. That's a stretch.
I was going to be the Goodrich tire guy, but I used that one last year.

OK, one more thing. Any advice for your fans?
Be true to yourself.

computers

 Before Nintendo

Published "quasiennially," **REIGN OF TOADS** *provides a voice for a generation that has grown up with computers but feels as alienated as anyone else by the explosion of technology. "Reign of Toads is about how things would logically proceed if not for people trying to make a lot of money and throwing things off course," says editor Kyle Silfer. One issue contains thoughts on the boundary between stealing an image and making it your own; another offers tips on getting connected to the Internet using thrifted computers. "Before Nintendo" is excerpted from Kyle's introduction to issue 3.*

I was in sixth grade when the first home computer came into existence, the Radio Shack TRS-80 Model I, Level I, a pathetic two-piece job with 4K of RAM, crude built-in BASIC, a cassette tape drive for data storage and retrieval, a black-and-white television in "custom" plastic housing, and two games (blackjack and backgammon). It sold like hotcakes. My father was a math teacher who spearheaded a student drive to collect funds to buy one. The school itself wasn't interested until he started the ball rolling. Then they bought them and kept buying them. There were TRS-80s everywhere in the building. Now they are dinosaurs. Extinct.

My existence precedes Nintendo. My existence precedes Atari. My existence precedes Space Invaders. I used to play pinball machines with bells on them and mechanical score displays that chugged like assembly-line drill presses when you pressed the button to start your game. I remember two five-ball games for twenty-five cents, then one five-ball game for twenty-five cents, then the newfangled digital machines and two *three-ball* games for a quarter. Now, of course, you're lucky to get *one* three-ball game for that price. Fifty cents is more like it. I even remember this sleazy penny arcade in a half-ruined amusement park at Pine Lake, New York, where my parents sent me on the bus to take swimming lessons with all these kids who hated me. But let me tell you: there were *ten-cent* machines there. Two *five*-ball games for *ten cents*. Ancient, dusty engines of entertainment with dim flashing orange lights and a manual plunger so you could pump as many balls into play as you wanted. All these "card game" theme machines like "Aces Wild!" or "Jack O' Diamonds" or "Royal Flush!" And pinball was just the half of it. These weird target-shooting games left over from some unknown era of popularity, little plastic animals with light detector sensors nailed to their sides and cardboard cutouts that swooped and rattled across the art deco backdrop while you pumped away with a noisy, sparking, sawed-off shotgun with nonfunctioning sight. Then there was this construction game where you controlled a large red metal bulldozer and pushed dried beans across a glass tank. These were contrivances of unparalleled mechanical genius. I swear to God, people will look back on the few remaining artifacts in fifty years and they'll be like the fucking pyramids. I have no doubt in my mind that every single one of those machines has been landfilled or sold for scrap.

Anyone born in the temporal epicenter around 1967 knows stuff like this. Anyone born later doesn't because it wasn't there anymore. I had a conversation with my grandfather once about how he could remember a significant amount of time when there were no automobiles. That is unfathomable now except in a strange, science fiction sort of way. I believe that the slacker generation stands in a similar position with regard to digital technology and mass media meltdown. We remember no home computers. We remember no CDs. We remember the world before MTV made or broke presidents. But, like my grandfather, only just barely. Only in our youth. We are the last of the pre-digital citizens, and we have surfed the wave so well that we fit right in with the rest of the techno youth, like well-adjusted foster children.

"Solve it Yourself" JFK Assassination Diorama

All the Zapruder films, Oliver Stone projects, and worn out copies of *Six Seconds Over Dallas* have never allowed Americans literally to reconstruct for themselves the fateful events of November 22, 1963. Now for the first time ever *Verbivore* is proud to afford you the tools to judge for yourself. Did Oswald act alone? Rearrange and add pieces upon our 3-D Dealey Plaza diorama until your morbid fascination is satisfied.

1 The Presidential motorcade. As Texas governor John Connally contemplated the ravioli he had spilled in his sock, the Presidential motorcade hurtled toward its rendezvous with history. Ravioli or roulette???

2 Lee Harvey Oswald. A desperate man acting alone out of his love for the KGB, *or* an obscene android operated by Richard Nixon? (Nixon was, after all, in Dallas that day at a Pepsi stockholders convention.) [Place figure behind Book Depository.]

3 Abraham Zapruder and Marilyn Monroe. Was Zapruder's production of the most famous evidence in the case in fact a canny cover-up for his own insane jealousy of Kennedy's famous tryst? Zapruder is alleged to have seen "Some Like it Hot" 57 times between 1960 and 1963.

4 Fidel Castro. A one-time baseball star in Cuba, Castro vigorously opposed Kennedy's support of the proposed Designated Hitter Rule. Castro's possible involvement in the assassination at any rate forestalled implementation of the controversial rule for sixteen years.

5 Alien spacecraft. The military elite has long suppressed the relationship the Kennedy White House had established with the leaders of the peaceful planet Viirgblåt. Hours after the assassination, lcal winos reported the appearance of a large pie plate in the Dallas sky. [Hang figure through string over desk lamp, as shown.]

6 Abraham Lincoln: Shot in a theater, whose assassin then hid in a "book depository." Did he arrive too late?

A The Texas State Book Depository. From which some bullets were fired at President Kennedy.

B The Greek-revival colonnade behind the Grassy Knoll. Until this structure is disassembled and subjected to a rigorous battery of electrochemical tests, we may never know its secrets.

C The wall separating the parking lot from Dealey Plaza, behind which Oliver Stone imagines he saw Joe Pesci.

D The inescapable double arch ruthlessly governs the entire shape of American culture.

conspiracies

The Verbivore JFK Assassination Diorama

Sure, you can retrace Lee Harvey Oswald's steps. You can memorize the Warren Commission report. You can conduct your own ballistics tests. But why? Jeremy Braddock and Miguel Echegaray of **VERBIVORE** *have done the research for you. "This exercise will make more sense to anyone who's had a chance to wander around Dealey Plaza and been* accosted by people selling you newsletters, books, and, above all, their opinions," explains Jeremy, who launched his zine of "cultural criticism and victual reality" in 1994. "The assassination is only interesting as long as no one believes the truth can ever be known."

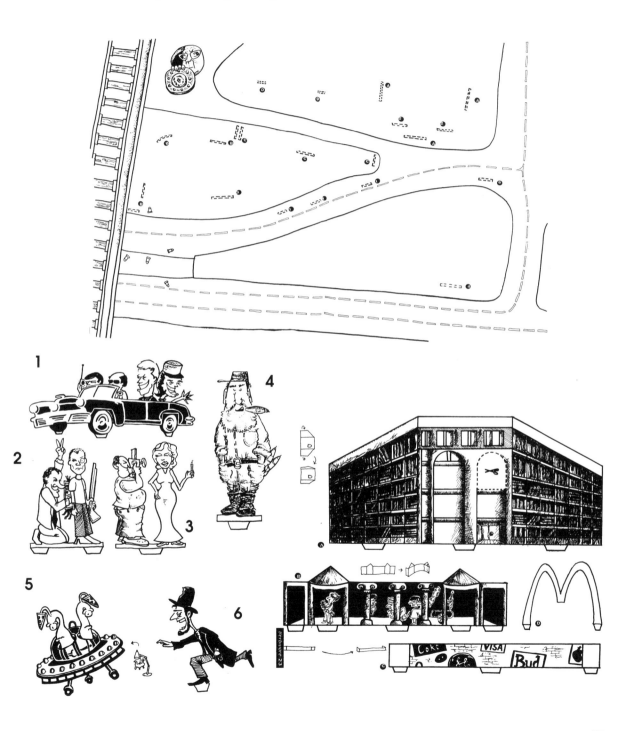

dating

Mystery Date: An Appreciation

$1.00

Mystery Date

#2

ONE GAL'S GUIDE TO GOOD STUFF

*After Lynn Peril wrote this essay to introduce her zine of nostalgia, **MYSTERY DATE**, many readers shared their own happy recollections of the game. For one male friend, however, the article stirred only painful memories: His childhood neighbors, the Trenelli twins, played "Mystery Date" often and made him dress as each of the dates.*

As you should have noticed by now, this publication is called *Mystery Date* (at least until the Milton Bradley legal department catches up with me). In the mid-sixties I was but one of millions of little girls lusting after the board game of the same name. Think back, or if you're not old enough to remember, just trust me, okay? It's Saturday morning and you're watching cartoons with your older brother when a commercial blasts its way into your subconscious:

"Mystery Date, are you ready for your mystery date? Don't be late, it must be great, so open the door for your . . . mystery date," a bland male singer warbles while a group of frenzied pre-pubescents gather around a game board. "Get Mystery Date, the great new game of fun and romance," intones the announcer. The pre-pubescents squeak and yip. "Is he a dream . . . or is he a dud?" Oh, the heady excitement of it all! Gentle reader, I wanted it. I wanted it with a singular, devoted, unwavering desire. You know, the hold-my-breath-until-I-turn-blue-unless-I-get-it desire that we don't usually carry into adulthood.

What materialized that coming Christmas, however, was a "Campus Queen" lunch box. A lunch box! Had the adults misunderstood me? Or—and this just may be it—did I simply assume that the shimmering aura of my want would tip them off, so I never actually mentioned it? For twenty-six long, hard years I was without the game, until last year, when sympathetic friends bought me both the 1965 and the 1972 editions.

For those of you unacquainted with "Mystery Date," the object is to be ready for your date when you open the door. (Look, I know some of you are wondering about the gender-specific socialization inherent in a game that teaches girls to be ready on time for their boyfriends. I also know you're wondering if there was a similar game for boys—one in which the object is, perhaps, to leave the toilet seat down after using it. To my knowledge, the answer is no.) The goal involves collecting cards printed with various accessories necessary to go on either a formal dance date, bowling date, beach date, or ski date. For example, you might draw a card with a ski sweater or another with bowling shoes.

The genius behind this game comes when it's time to open the plastic "Mystery Door." Behind the door is a photographic image of either the Beach Date (in shorts and Hawaiian shirt); the Ski Date (in form-fitting ski pants); the Formal Date (in white dinner jacket and red carnation—could that be a corsage for you in the box he's holding?); or the Bowling Date (who, for some reason, looks like a Future CPA of America).

There is also "The Dud." Dressed in a thermal undershirt and work pants and boots, he is supposed to be the "bad date," the one who will cause a player to "lose valuable time getting rid of him." I can see the look on the face of the Milton Bradley designer who worked on "Mystery Date," opening the door to his daughter's first boyfriend and realizing that she, like millions of girls, imprinted on the Dud. (Then again, I might just be scrambling for an excuse for more than one past relationship: "I couldn't help it—I was imprinted on the Dud!") Milton Bradley eventually eliminated the Dud in response to the complaints of mothers who believed their sons resembled him.

So there you are—you've opened the door to find Mr. Ski Date waiting, and, horror of horrors, you're holding a bathing suit, formal bag and shoes, and a parka. Damn. You roll the die to move around the game board, picking up, discarding, and swapping accessory cards and opening the door. The first girl to open the door to the appropriate date while holding the proper accessory cards wins!

Milton Bradley updated "Mystery Date" in 1972. No more pink and white box—now it's yellow and fuchsia. The rules remain the same. "The Dud" has become "The Pest," and "The Bowling Date" has disappeared everywhere but in the instructions. On the game board, we now have drawings of: the Beach Date (surfboard, snorkel, and aviator shades), the Ski Date (in flared ski pants—the thrill is gone), the Formal Dance Date (purple tux with bell-bottom pants and platform shoes), and the Bicycle Date (maybe they figured since "bowling" and "bicycling" both begin with B, no one would notice). Once again, "The Pest" isn't as bad as he's cracked up to be, especially since he's the only one not wearing flared pants.

What was the appeal of "Mystery Date"? It was tailor-made for girls going through that hideous first flush of adolescence when everybody looks weird, with braces and glasses and bodies that grow too much in one direction and not enough in another, and everyone begins to wonder, "Am I normal?" Of course, by placing all the emphasis on looks and the all-important boyfriend, these games also had the potential to make awkward social retards like me feel even more alienated.

There is a poetic justice to all this. Recently I bought a "Barbie—Queen of the Prom" game ($4) from a guy on the street, who told me, "Be sure to play it with boys, because it's all about getting boyfriends." I knew then that he and his boyfriends had each imagined himself as Queen of the Prom. The drip of candle wax on the game board told me they must have made a real night of it, chips and dip, maybe hot cocoa. And I knew we were sisters under the skin, making up stories of the adolescence that we, the misfits, never had.

Don'ts for Boys

From the first page of the first issue of **BUST***, Betty Boob and Celina Hex have been reminding readers that being a girl is cool. "It's excellent super fun to say yes to cute boys, yes to wild car rides, and yes to life." Their themed issues have explored sex (featuring an eye-opening article about puppy lust), growing up female, fashion and beauty, bad girls, and "men we love." The latter included this classic guide for boys, written by Betty, Ms. M., John-boy, and Jimmie-a-go-go.*

Issue # 6 Summer / Fall 1995 $2.50

Men We Love

Thurston Moore

Iggy Pop

Jon Stewart

Keanu Reeves

Henry Rollins

& lots of girls on boys

Does the term "boy disease" mean anything to you? It's not a love-hate thing; it's a love-crazy thing. If only boys would follow some simple rules, to help girls avoid this horrible virus.

In the Beginning . . .

- Don't wait. If you like me, ask me out. We're not in high school anymore. If I like you, I'll ask you out.
- Don't bother with "I'll call" if we go on a date and it doesn't go well. Leave, gracefully.
- Don't think it means I want a ring if we fuck on the first date.
- Don't lie. I'll catch you.
- Don't not call when you say you're going to call. Because otherwise I will wait for your call and that's not nice.
- Don't play footsie during dinner and then pretend nothing happened.
- Don't tell my friends that you think I'm special unless you mean it. If you tell my friends, they tell me. I end up thinking you're special for thinking I'm special. Then when you don't do anything to follow up I'll be forced to realize you're not.
- Don't use being drunk as an excuse for "accidentally" kissing me. If you kiss me, drunk or not, you have a BIG KISS to deal with.
- Don't call me if you haven't gotten over your last girlfriend or mother. I'm not an understudy for a psycho-romantic drama.
- Don't monopolize the conversation. Asking questions is very attractive.
- Don't use the "I'm-not-ready-for-a-relationship" excuse. I'll think you're trying to get rid of me with stale stock lines.
- Don't screen my calls. It's creepy.
- Don't pretend to like me in order to fuck me. If you want to fuck me, tell me. I can always use a boy toy.
- Don't tell me that you want to spend the weekend with me and bail out at 10:30 on a Thursday night. Worse, do not skip calling me to bail. The latter is deception, which does not allow for resolution of feelings.
- Don't be afraid to fall in like with me, you big baby.
- Don't kiss and tell. But because I know you will, you slob, do me the favor of not degrading me. Mention that I'm cool, funny, and smart and that you're super lucky to even be telling your friend about my naked action.
- Don't be afraid of falling in like with me just because I live in a different city. Long-distance romances have their advantages. We don't have to get married, we don't have to see each other all the time, it allows sexual freedom and don't forget the anticipation.

The Relationship

- Don't pester me with lame questions like, "Where is this relationship going?" A relationship is a dynamic form of expression, not two lost motorists.
- Don't freak out when you ring me up at 3 A.M. my time and I am not there. It does not mean I am having sex with someone.
- Don't go on tour with your stupid band and call me when you feel like it.
- Don't borrow my car to cheat on me. I don't want to make payments on the source of a painful memory.
- Don't tell me you were drunk and don't know how you ended up in some girl's bed naked with two used condoms on the floor.

- Don't call me a jealous freak and then act all jealous when you see me cracking up with other boys.
- Don't tell me you are having lunch with her so you wouldn't hurt her feelings. You're not that nice, she's not that weak, and I'm not that stupid.
- Don't come home from vacation with hickeys, strange underwear, a box of condoms with a bunch missing, or scratches on your back. Do come home from vacation lovesick for me with a big present and a bouncy hard-on.
- Don't squeeze my juicy butt at parties to prove you own me. Squeeze it at home to prove you want me.
- Don't forget to introduce me to your friends, unless you know I won't like them. In that case, thanks.
- Don't try to get the waitress's phone number while I'm at the table, or wait until I go to the bathroom and then break up with me when I come back.
- Don't show all the naked pictures of me you've taken to your loser friends.
- Don't pretend you were out with the boys last night when I know you weren't.
- Don't act like we never talked about going to the Virgin Isles together. I'm rarely given to complete delusion.
- Don't order me diet food while I am in the bathroom. Order me cake. Something with chocolate fudge would be great.
- Don't tell me not to get hysterical, not to overreact, that I'm imagining things, that I'm on the rag.
- Don't forget my birthday, for Chrissakes.
- Don't raise your voice or I will only want to remain silent while you lose control of yourself.
- Don't tell me in an exasperated tone that you have told her over and over again never to call.

Sex
- Don't believe that women don't like doing it.
- Don't ever fuck me, come inside me, and then say "I gotta go," cause if you do, you'd better.
- Don't fuck me on Sunday and not call me till Wednesday. Call me on Monday. Remember this little rhyme: SunDay called MonDay in OneDay.
- Don't touch all the good parts while I'm sleeping unless it's with intent to wake me.
- Don't keep saying your parents won't hear us.
- Don't ask me to fuck your friends. How would you like if I asked you to . . . wait a second.
- Don't ask me how many guys I've slept with. I can barely keep count sometimes.
- Don't ever try to have sex with me with your socks on. It makes me think of Woody Allen.
- "Don't touch" doesn't mean "Wait, touch."
- Don't forget that foreplay means the play before and play is fun.
- Don't forget that my nipples are not detachable, nor can they tune in Tokyo.
- Don't get uptight if I want to masturbate. Help or watch; it looks pretty cool.
- Don't ask me to count my orgasms after we do it.
- Don't tell me how any of your old girlfriends "did anything." Put that stupid shoe on the other foot and see how ugly it looks.
- Don't tell me I'm cute when I am trying to be sexy. Pay attention.
- Don't have sex while you're answering the phone.

- Don't say "Thanks, it was fun!"
- Don't use the following excuses to get out of spending the night with me: have to get up early; curfew; roommate may get lonely; must walk dog.
- Don't tell me to go down on you first if you are planning to absolutely not go down on me.
- Don't ask me to swallow anything you wouldn't swallow yourself.
- Don't tell me that condoms: don't fit; don't feel good; make you break out.
- Don't watch TV during sex unless it's porn.
- Don't ask me if you're the best; it's not a contest.
- Don't tell me this won't hurt.
- Don't tell me you can pull out in time.
- Don't tell me I'm not wet enough, like it's an insult.
- Don't ever ask me if my trip to the gynecologist is a turn-on.
- Don't insist on videotaping our sexcapades. If you want to make me your fucking co-star, ask me if I'd like the part.
- Don't complain that girls have too many rules.

FREE ADVICE

"Don't hide your creativity, and don't hide yourself, except maybe now and then to be polite. Who knows, maybe you'll change someone's mind. Remember Gandhi's line: What you are doing may not seem important, but it's extremely important that you do it."

—Bob Bellerue, Basura

decline

Hope I Die Before Marcia Gets Old

In issue 3 of **BUST**, *the zine for women too old for* Sassy, *editors Betty Boob and Celina Hex welcomed their first submission from a guy, Edward Berridge, who wrote from Australia to profess his admiration and share his thoughts on aging.*

I would never have thought of myself as part of a generation at all if it were not that whenever I meet someone roughly my own age I can always break the ice with a comment about "The Brady Bunch." And now we are, as a generation, getting old. Indeed, the aging process is a horrific and irredeemable notion. First there is the physical deterioration. Men, for example, go soft around the gut. It becomes a major life hassle to maintain tone. You get lines on your face and see your friends losing hair—all those expressions of bodily decay which we know leads to (let's capitalize this, cause it's important) DEATH.

But aging is more than just looking older. There is also that whole trip of *feeling* older. I notice, for instance, that my hangovers are worse these days and I need a day's rest to get over them. I have to exercise constantly to achieve the sort of suppleness I took for granted ten years ago. As you age, time begins to fly. It idles, rolls slowly out on the runway, taxis, picks up speed, and, before you know it, breaks the sound barrier. Suddenly you are older than most popular athletes, actors, musicians, and supermodels—and you realize you will never have their money or lifestyle. As a kid, you didn't resent famous people because you could still kid yourself that you would be like them when you grew up. You knew time was on your side. You had forever to make your move.

No, adulthood for most of us is a bad, bad let-down. You are older and poorer and dying, but worst of all, you are anonymous. You are not photographed, you are not interviewed, nobody cares what you think or what you are wearing. You are the sort of person who gets tickets too far away from the stage to see Madonna or U2. You have to queue up outside nightclubs and restaurants. You are never going to be famous (and I mean real fame, not Andy Warhol's fifteen minutes of fame. If you happen to see an accident and get interviewed, or if you are a game show contestant, that is not fame. That is a mockery of fame). We come to realize that our lives are drab and dirty, not only relative to the celebrity lives we read about but, more importantly, to the people we see on television.

The problem with our generation isn't that we cannot tell the difference between reality and television. Our problem is that we are too acutely aware of the difference. Reality fares badly in comparison, so we watch a lot of TV. Consider "Family Matters": The main character is a bus driver who lives in a huge, multi-bedroom home. (In reality, lawyers and management consultants live in mansions like that. On television, it's bus drivers.) In the real world, we cannot escape the suspicion that more or less all people are losers, including bus drivers. And one can only imagine that the son of a Minnesota accountant would be the king of losers in Beverly Hills. Yet on television, to be ordinary is to be jolly, affluent, and fulfilled.

So . . . what in fact? Who knows? Having postulated some tenuous connection between us on the grounds of a shared Brady Bunch viewing experience, let me apologize for any incoherence. I consider myself more of a writer of fiction than an essayist. Well, in fact, I am not any sort of writer at all. I have cupboards of short stories and rejection slips, but that does not, of course, make a person a writer. I am just a market researcher. But we will all be fifty soon and need each other more than ever.

deviants

Family Circus of Horrors

Will Pfeifer couldn't breathe—his head was filled with pop culture debris and he couldn't breathe. So he dumped it all into **UNDERBELLY**. *Besides examining "The Family Circus," Will has taken a closer look at the cross-dressing, time-traveling, long-suffering Superman sidekick Jimmy Olsen; detailed the sordid history of infomercials and the minor celebrities who populate them; and analyzed the watershed teen nudie flick,* Private School for Girls.

The 3/7/95 strip proved what some of us knew all along about *The Family Circus:* It's the greatest work-in-progress by a comics genius since Robert Crumb killed off Fritz the Cat. For those of you who missed it, the ever-whimsical circle was divided that day into two panels: In the first, Jeffy is asleep, happily dreaming about Bill Griffith's postmodern comic strip character, Zippy the Pinhead (!). In the second, Mommy wakes him up and, sleepy-eyed, he asks her, "Why did you turn it off, Mommy? I was watching Zippy the Pinhead."

Just what is going on here?

When I saw this strip, I looked at it again and again. My mind could not process the information. Lovable Jeffy sharing panel space with surreal Zippy (drawn by Griffith, incidentally)? *The Family Circus* has long had a reputation as the strangest strip on the funny pages, and this should erase all doubts. Let's face it, kommixx folk, it's time to reevaluate the unsung genius of the funnies, the heir to Ernie Bushmiller's throne . . . Mister Bil Keane.

"Why did you turn it off, Mommy? I was watchin' 'Zippy the Pinhead.'"

Of course, a lil ol' zinester like me isn't the first guy to recognize Keane's brilliance. Mini-comics godfather Steve Willis has been analyzing Keane's work for years. Willis says he launched "The Bil Keane Watch" in the now-defunct *City Limits Gazette* because *The Family Circus* seemed so mundane. But he soon found hidden meanings and repeated symbols that added a fascinating subtext to the antics of Billy, Dolly, and the gang. Sure, everyone knows about "Not Me," dead grandpa, and Billy's intricate trips around the neighborhood. But ever notice how all the kids have one giant nostril? How about that none of the telephone poles have any wires? (Willis says this is most common in strips about death, making them handy metaphors for Christianity, but I've seen them in jokey strips, too.) Clearly, there's more at work here than meets the (simple, dot-like) eye.

One night a few months ago, a friend and I were at a bar discussing junk culture when I brought up *The Family Circus*. My friend mentioned that he had been browsing around a Goodwill store a few days before and came across an album filled with old *Family Circus* panels. I stopped by Goodwill. There it was. A cheap, jaundiced album filled with Keane panels from 1981 to 1983. I have no idea who put it together. All I know is that if I bought this thing in search of Keanesian weirdness, I was rewarded with the first strip in the book.

1/21/81: While Mommy puts away dishes in the background, Billy pages through what's apparently a book about where babies come from. There's a fairly large, realistic drawing of a baby curled up in a womb. Billy, wearing the patented Keane blasé expression (a line drawn across his eye so only the bottom half can be seen) remarks in his best kids-say-the-darnedest-things manner, "Bet I know what babies like about being born. They can stretch." Mommy, needless to say, is a bit surprised by Billy's reading material. Who gave him this book? Was it Daddy, trying to avoid that little talk? The aspect of the picture that should have gotten Billy's attention, namely that the baby-to-be-born has a normal, human head and not a freakishly flattened one like Billy's, isn't mentioned.

As I soon discovered, this wasn't the first time Billy had confronted the question, "Where did I come from?" Apparently on some of those meandering walks around the neighborhood, someone told Billy about the birds and bees. In the 1/12/81 strip (which is after the 1/21/81 strip—who put this album together?), the family is enjoying dinner when Billy proudly says, "Wanna hear a funny one? In sex ed today [sex ed? at his age?] a kid said his father thinks STORKS bring babies." No one is shocked at Billy's carnal knowledge; in fact, this time Mommy is wearing the blasé expression and, as always, Daddy remains an enigma behind those opaque glasses of his. So Billy's not the innocent he appears to be (in the 2/7/81 strip, according to Dolly, he says "an X-rated word" while building one of those crate-and-roller skate scooters no one ever really built). But that's appropriate, because the world of *The Family Circus* isn't as innocent as it appears, either.

'Bet I know what babies like about being born.
They can stretch.''

Unlike the worldly Billy, Jeffy (whose age was established as three in the 3/1/95 strip) constantly questions the world around him. Big brother Billy should take him aside and set him straight on the birds and bees, 'cause Jeffy's confused. In the 7/12/83 strip, Jeffy brings a jar-encased insect to Mommy and asks "Mommy, is this grasshopper a boy or a girl?" Awwww. Cute, right? If only things were always so innocent. In the 6/25/83 strip, during a trip to the beach, Jeffy asks, "Is that lady wearing her WHOLE bathing suit, Mommy?" Most disturbingly, in the 5/6/83 strip, a tearful Jeffy cries, "I bit my tongue, Mommy! Will you kiss it?" I don't want to think about the implications of Jeffy's request, except to say that Freud had a name for that complex and it rhymes with "incredible."

And what about those parents? Though we have no idea what Daddy does for a living or how Mommy keeps her figure after three kids, we do know the parents in *The Family Circus* are disciplinarians. In the 7/30/81 strip, Billy has broken a window playing baseball and a stern Mommy warns him, "You just wait until the designated hitter comes home." Yikes! In the 6/6/81 strip, a furious Mommy (hands on hips, classic comic strip parental anger pose) demands of the four children, "Who called me 'Mommy Dearest'?" Apparently she's earned that nickname, because in

24

the 5/10/81 strip, we see her angrily pounding on a door as the ever-witty Billy says, "If she won't come out, let's fire tear gas through the window." Sure, Billy's probably just imitating some fake cop show he saw on their fake TV (it's got no cord), but who knows?

There's so much more to discuss: those ghostly imps "Not Me," "Ida Know," and "Fuck You" (okay, I made that one up), the spectral visage of dead grandpa, a dog named "Barfy" (what's that all about?), the awkward religious references, not to mention the kids celebrating birthdays and holidays like clockwork but never getting older. But all that's spooky and fascinating about *The Family Circus* can be summed up in my all-time favorite comic strip. And I don't mean just my fave *Family Circus* strip—I mean my favorite comic strip of all time. It's been hanging above my drawing table ever since it first ran on 9/23/90.

"If she won't come out, let's fire tear gas through her window."

Keane skipped his usual Sunday formulas (Billy draws the strip, Billy takes a walk, everyone talks at once, the kids grow up, an old tree/house/school remembers children of days past, etc.) and went right for the jugular: Billy and Dolly are standing in a field overrun with weeds. Flies buzz around their heads. The sky is dark. A factory and some nearby houses belch smoke. A pickup in the distance spews more muck and blasts a loud "boom boom boom" music (rap?) as the driver tosses garbage from the window. A sickly green stream sits stagnant before the kids, filled with cans, tires, and rotting fish. A sign that reads "No Shooting" stands riddled with bullet holes. In the midst of this desolation, there is no clever remark from Billy. No innocently humorous "Dolly-isms." All Dolly, wearing a world-weary variation of the blasé expression, can ask is this:

"Why do babies leave heaven to come here?"

I have no idea what to make of this strip. Did Jean-Paul Sartre write it? Is it a pro-abortion strip? A pro-birth control strip? It's definitely the bleakest thing I've ever seen in the Sunday funnies, and that includes the glory days of *Peanuts*, when Charles Schulz examined the pain of childhood in excruciating detail. This is way beyond that.

I do have a theory. Unlike in other strips, the telephone poles in this strip have wires. Maybe Keane is implying that Billy and Dolly have stepped out of their idyllic comic world and entered our own. Maybe he's saying that what they saw was so horrible it led them to question the existence and/or wisdom of God. Maybe he's saying comic strip kids like Billy and Dolly would rather never be born than live in our world.

Or maybe I'm just reading too much into *The Family Circus*.

Real Life Giant Construction Equipment for Kids

You never know what to expect from **HITCH***, Rod Lott's journal of pop culture absurdity. For one of his regular "He-Man Adventures," for example, he attended a seminar by the manufacturer of ErecAid. You place your droopy penis in this vacuum pump and . . . oh, never mind. Recent issues have also included fast-food horror stories (if you can't suck your milkshake through the straw, stop trying), David Hasselhoff gun targets, and Rod's thoughts on dozens of obscure videos, including "Real Life Giant Construction Equipment for Kids." "I thought it would be funny to review," Rod says, "but it was horrifying."*

At the beginning of this educational video, which I purchased for $4.95 through a Sunday coupon circular, two young boys are walking around a dilapidated junkyard scattered with chunks of rock on which they might crack their skulls. The oldest, Max, tells the younger, Alex: "See that big yellow monster over there? That's a 520-horsepower D-10 bulldozer. Big as a house!" This is the first clue that Alex is destined for a traumatic adolescence.

Exploring the site, the pair stumbles on a beat-up Thermos. Max warns Alex not to open it because it might be filled with "rotten, stinky chicken soup." It contains worse medicine: Hard Hat Harry, a "genie" with buff biceps who remarks upon his release, "Man, I gotta get a bigger Thermos!" (Don't we all.)

Grateful for his freedom, Harry grants the boys three wishes. And just what do these two eager, enterprising, red-blooded youths wish for? Pogs? Money? Whores? Nope—they blow the opportunity of a lifetime to see *construction equipment*. Harry sprinkles them with "magic gravel," and—poof—they're transported to a building site.

Real Life GIANT CONSTRUCTION EQUIPMENT For Kids ~ DELUXE EDITION ~ Featuring... "Hard Hat Harry™!"

FREE ADVICE

"Don't start a music zine. There are already ten thousand music zines out there. Nobody cares what you think about music anyway."
—Mark Frauenfelder, *bOING bOING*

26

There, the boys are introduced to digging, drilling, and dumping machines, each of which, eerily, can speak. A back hoe front loader sounds like Elvis, a road-paver mimics Dracula, and a dumptruck talks like Arnold Schwarzenegger. Another dumptruck, this one with a Jersey accent, openly ridicules the boys. Even worse, the young innocents are subjected to a barrage of sexual innuendo. It is introduced in an ever-so-subtle fashion as Hard Hat Harry talks of the time it takes "to erect the tower crane." Then Pete the Piledriver explains how his support beams "keep the pile from moving when I slam into it [with my] king-sized hammer." Just before breaking into song, a crane boasts how "me and my crane friends can do it all day long, and we never get tired."

Harry becomes party to the perversion when he forces Max and Alex to watch a dumptruck "back up and dump its heavy load." The dumptruck croons, "Fill me up and tap my load!" A concrete pumper explains, "I use them for stability so I won't tip over when I'm pumping" just before he is interrupted by the arriving ready-mix truck. "I'm going to pour my concrete into your rear hamper," it says. "Watch my chute come out. Ready, aim, fire!" The pumper elaborates: "Then the concrete worker pulls my snaking hose. When he gives the signal, I take a deep breath and blow that concrete out at a stupendous rate!"

The height of the grotesque talk comes when the paver receives its asphalt. "Ah," it says, pleased, "just the way I like it: Hot and wet! Between two to four inches is the ideal depth." Is it an accident that most of these paving machines are manufactured by a company called Wacker?

By the time Harry tells the boys he likes to call the bucket trucks "cherry pickers," it's too late: The boys have been corrupted. When older and wiser Max spots a female construction worker waving at him, he says with a knowing leer, "Ask her if I can have a bite of her sandwich!"

That night, after returning home, Max and Alex giggle with pleasure, remembering they have two more wishes. Given Harry's corrupting influence, we can only assume they will include more monster machinery. Only if the trio had been visited by Killdozer could this video be more fun.

HITCH
#7 • JUNE / JULY 1995 • $3.50
FIRST ANNIVERSARY ISSUE!

FEATURING:
• Oscar Suck!
• Up Close with Crispin Glover!
• El Chico Prank!
• Free Joycelyn Elders Board Game!
• Free Fag Milkcaps, Too!

25 Years of Planet of the Apes
Damn Dirty Apes!

---

disasters

The Great Boston Molasses Flood

No zine covers the B-side of pop culture better than **MURDER CAN BE FUN**. *Its editor, "mild-mannered civil servant" John Marr, is an expert at rooting absurdities from mayhem, and vice versa. "I started* Murder Can Be Fun *in 1986 to provide a sordid outlet for my more unhealthy obsessions," he says. For one memorable piece of journalism, "Death at Disneyland," John scrolled through the decades of archived newspapers to compile an alternately bone-chilling and hilarious run-down of people who have been killed in accidents at the theme park. He later gave the same treatment to zoos, teaching by way of several horrifying examples that polar bears are not warm and cuddly when you climb into their cages drunk in the middle of the night. This retelling of one of America's strangest disasters first appeared in issue 11.*

Wanna play, Buster?

NAUGHTY CHILDREN

FREE ADVICE

"(1) Get your zine into Ulrich's International Periodical Directory. Claim a subscriber base of 1.7 million. Don't ever say that you accept poetry on your submission to Ulrich's, however, even as a joke, because for years you'll get bad poetry that could possibly cause internal hemorrhaging if it weren't for the accompanying SASEs to be used at your discretion. (2) Work at Kinko's. (Better yet, ask a friend to.) (3) Remember, the sloppier the finished product, the more street cred you have. (4) Keep other bad zines lying around for when you get the monthly request for a free copy from a weasel who 'may' subscribe."

—Jeff Hansen, X Magazine

The Great Boston ≡

≡*MOLASSES FLOOD*

For sheer strangeness, no disaster has ever topped
Boston's Great Molasses Flood. Other disasters have
run up higher body counts, caused more damage, inspired
books & movies, & are remembered as Important Historical
Events. The Molasses Flood was none of these: a mere
21 dead & $1 million damages, it's only been the subject
of a handful of obscure magazine articles & newspaper
clippings. Historically, it's peanuts, not even worthy
of a footnote. But the idea & irony of 2½ million gallons
of molasses raging through city streets, knocking over
buildings & killing people in the middle of January ...
unbeatable.

The date was January 15, 1919. At the intersection
of Foster & Commercial streets in Boston's North End,
the Purity Distilling Co. had a large, riveted steel
storage tank, 50' high & 90' diameter. The tank stored
shipments of raw molasses received from Cuba & the West
Indies. The molasses would then be pumped from the tank
into rail cars bound for a distillery in Cambridge which
produced industrial-grade alcohol for the munitions industry. On that particular day, the tank was almost
full, holding 2.3 million gallons of molasses weighing
over 27 million pounds. Although cloudy, the weather
was unseasonably warm for a Boston winter: 44°F with light
winds.

At 12:41, it happened. Most people heard nothing;
others remember a low rumbling or a sharp tearing sound.
The two bottom rows of plates on the tank tore open,
unleashing a 20' high wave of molasses moving some 35 mph
onto the unsuspecting streets of the North End.

The conductor of the elevated train near the tank
probably spotted it first. He rounded the curve & then
"All I could see was molasses rushing toward me". He
managed to stop the train in time.

Less lucky were those in the neighboring buildirgs.
A local boxer, asleep in a 3rd floor bedroom "awoke in
several feet of molasses", which drowned (suffocated?)
his mother downstairs. The firemen in the nearby stat-
ionhouse were in a similar predicament. "We bumped our
heads on the floor above trying to keep our noses &
mouths above the fluid". One evidently didn't, & drowned.

When the molasses hit, it hit with power. The tank
tore apart with such force that huge sections of the steel
plates were flung up to 200'. Several chunks hit the el

Old Dan Tucker came to town
He swallered a hogshead o' lasses down
The 'lasses worked and the hogshead burst
And off went Tucker in a thundergust.

AFTER THE TANK OF MOLASSES BLEW UP.

track columns like shrapnel, shearing one & almost knocking down the others so that a few sections of the track
fell to the ground.

The molasses itself was capable of knocking things
about, too. Many wooden buildings were torn from their
foundations, and bobbed like corks on the flood. 14 were
completely destroyed. The flood even knocked one guy
clean into the harbor, where he was rescued by a passing
tug.

But he was one of the lucky ones. The worst thing
about the flood was that it was molasses -- thick gooey
sticky molasses that stuck to everything, and everyone,
it touched, & would not let go. The Boston Post described it perfectly: "There was no escape from the wave.
Human and animal alike could not flee. Snared in its
flood was to be stifled. Once it smeared a head -- human
or animal -- there was no coughing off the sticky mess.
To attempt to wipe it with hands was to make it worse.
Most of those who died, died of suffocation".

The molasses was like quicksand. Passers-by, wading
in to help stuck people, were themselves trapped. Horses
were hopeless, and had to be shot on the spot. People
couldn't get out until mid-afternoon when the molasses
finally settled, and when they got home, they had to
cut their clothes off. According to the Boston Evening
Transcript, "The entire neighborhood is a sea of molasses"

Another reporter described the aftermath as "the
biggest mess since the Augean Stables". Cleaning up a

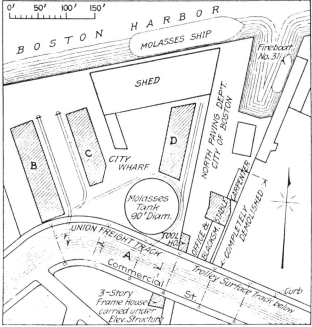

FIG. 1. LAYOUT OF DEVASTATED REGION NEAR
MOLASSES TANK

spill of over 2 million gallons of molasses is not an
easy job. It took a week just to recover the bodies
of the 21 victims. Molasses had to be pumped out of
every basement & washed into the harbor, a process that
took several months & turned the harbor brown. The
neighborhood reeked of molasses for weeks, and bystand-
ers and spectators succeeded in tracking molasses throughout the greater Boston area. Sticky trolley seats were
reported in Worcester, 45 miles away.

The press immediatly seized upon the idea of a "molasses explosion"; somehow, the molasses had fermented,
possibly due to the unseasonable warmth, and the resulting
alcohol explosively ignited by a careless cigarette.
Even Scientific American speculated along these lines.
A professor from Trinity College submitted the "Dan Tucker"
stanza (from an old folk song) to the Literary Digest,
claiming that it demonstrated that "the explosive potent-
ialities of molasses were recognized a long, long time
ago".

Of course, this isn't what happened. The tank had
a nice big vent in the roof that would have dissapated
the force of any explosion on top of the molasses. But
consider a bomb deeply submerged in the molasses, prefer-
ably placed by anarchists that were rife among the Italian
population of the North End -- now that has some possibilities.

FIG. 5. STEEL SHELL AND ELEVATED RAILWAY WRECKED

This was Purity's main defense against the 119 lawsuits filed against it in the wake of the flood. It did sound better than their other theories, blaming vibrations from the el or progessive weakness resulting from some earlier freight car collisions. It was feasible -- a good heavy bomb with a waterproof fuse would do the job nicely. It sounded possible. Remember, this was Sacco & Vanzetti country, where bomb throwing anarchists lurked, in the popular imagination, on every streetcorner. Purity was having some labor problems at the time, and claimed that posters threatening company property had been posted around the North End in the weeks prior to the flood.

The Massachusets Fire Prevention Commisioner took a somewhat more orthodox position. In a report issued a few months after the flood, he blamed it on simple structural inadequacy of the tank.

Then, it was to the courts for a masterpiece of litigation: $4\frac{1}{2}$ years and 40,000 transcript pages proving "they've got experts, we've got experts". For every MIT or Harvard professor Purity trotted out who swore high & low that it had to have been a bomb, the state produced a professor of their own saying that the tank simply broke because it wasn't strong enough. The judge (aka auditor) summed it up as: "I have listened to men upon the faith of whose judgement any capitalist might well rely in the expenditure of millions in structural steel swear that the secondary stresses in this kind of structure were negligible, & I have heard from equally authoratative sources that these same secondary stresses were the cause of the accident. Amid this swirl of polemical scientific waters it is not strange that the auditor has at times felt that the only rock to which he could safely cling was the obvious fact that at least $\frac{1}{2}$ the scientists must be wrong".

FIG. 6. STEEL PLATES WRAPPED AROUND COLUMN

The wrong half, of course, were the bomb theorists on the side of Purity. In building the tank, Purity had really screwed up. The company treasurer ordered a 2.3 million gallon tank with a factor of safety of 3 from the Hammond Iron Co., leaving the actual design up to them. No engineer at Purity ever checked the plans. The examiner at the Boston Building Department admitted that analyzing such a structure was beyond him, so he approved it because a civil engineer, presumably employed by Purity, had signed off on the plans. But this engineer had only done the foundation work; he hadn't even looked at the actual tank structure.

Using the unchecked plans, Hammond then proceeded to build a tank with plates thinner than called for. The end result was a tank with a safety factor well under the specified level. Even the defense experts agreed that they wouldn't have let that tank design by.

In the face of this, the judge was not impressed with Purity's other evidence of an anarchist bomb: a witness who claimed to have seen smoke (from a waterproof fuse, of course) rising from the tank shortly before the flood, and the results of bombs planted in scale models of the tank. He found the cause to be "high primary stresses, the low factor of safety, and the secondary stresses, in combination...". Purity reportedly wound up paying out some $1 million in damage claims.

Besides, if the anarchists had <u>really</u> wanted to put on a show, complete with fireworks & <u>real</u> property damage, they would have bombed the distillery over in Cambridge. Who ever heard of serious political radicals making a statement with molasses?

FREE ADVICE

"It's good to be conservative when distributing your zine. You never know who will plague you with the persistent question, 'Is this going to be in your zine?' It's awful to have people so conscious of their roles as characters. It's completely uninspiring."

—Linette Lao, *Crimewave U.S.A.*

<u>d r u g s</u>

Reptilian Thoughts

Jim Hogshire loves pills. They're colorful, bite-size, and effective. They're also so common that people take them for granted. To remedy that, Jim packs **PILLS-A-GO-GO** *with information about the tablets, capsules, syrups, powders, extracts, tinctures, and elixirs that soothe our aches, clear our passages, put us to sleep, keep us awake, and help us forget. Often Jim adds a footnote or two about unreported side effects, which can include arrest. In a bizarre case, Jim was busted in 1996 after police in Seattle raided his home and discovered "contraband"—two dried poppies purchased at a flower shop. On the way downtown, one cop asked, "With what you publish, weren't you expecting this?"*

This issue's pill review is devoted to a chemical called Dextromethorphan Hydrobromide. It's the DM in cough syrup, and one of the most mystifying of the drugs in the pharmacopoeia. Even though it is the king of over-the-counter cough medicines, it is barely mentioned in common reference works.

That's odd, since DM Hbr is related to some powerful anesthetics (like PCP). Sold all over the place to keep us away from codeine, it is strong enough to produce a strange high as well as convulsions, nausea, loss of consciousness, hypertension, and possible brain damage.

I drank about eight ounces of DM cough syrup, straight, no chaser. I was feeling kind of achy and wanted to see if it would kill pain. Earlier smaller doses had shown me that the stuff could cause confusion and restlessness, but I couldn't remember exactly how much I'd taken.

Soon any pain I had dissipated. After a few hours, I went to bed. It was midnight, but I felt neither awake nor asleep, sort of like a typical narcotic high but no great shakes. Mildly content, kind of nodding—just not as pleasant.

At four o'clock in the morning I awoke suddenly and remembered I had to go to Kinko's and also to shave off about a week's worth of stubble from my face. These ideas seemed very clear to me.

That seems normal enough except that I HAD A REPTILIAN BRAIN. My whole way of thinking and perceiving had changed. It was like I was operating with a medulla only or something.

I was able to do any mechanical thing just fine. I had full control over my motor functions but I still had the impression that I was ungainly. That's because I felt detached from my body, like being on laughing gas. So I got in the shower and shaved. While I was shaving I "thought" that for all I knew I was hacking my face to pieces. Since I didn't see any blood or feel any pain I didn't worry about it. In fact, my "feelings" were so shal-

PILLS-A-GO-GO
journal of pills

Spring 1995

#22

Do you love Vicodin?

Spring into Soma!

Celebrity Pills

Your favorite pill news from around the world

low or nonexistent that I couldn't have felt anything like anxiety. Looking back I see now I had lost any sense of time. I knew I was capable of performing various actions but I could not conceive of any consequences to those actions. Had I looked down and seen another limb, I wouldn't have been surprised at all. I would have just used it. It was very much like riding inside my own body.

I gained a kind of insight that I've only previously associated with acid or maybe dreams. In a dream, you aren't surprised by the absurd (an extra limb), and like on acid you realize the absurdity of it all. But there were no hallucinations.

The world became a binary place of dark/light, on/off, safety/danger. When I felt a need, I determined it was hunger and ate almonds until I didn't feel the need anymore. Same thing with water. It was like playing a game. Staying alive, but with no fear at all. I sat down and tried to write down how this felt so I could look at it later. I was very aware that I was stupid. I wrote down the word "Cro-Magnon." I probably seemed like Benny on "L.A. Law."

I thought I would have trouble driving but I had none. I only felt "unsafe" while in the dark street until I got into the "safe" car. Then I drove to Kinko's where I parked in the deserted street, felt quite content to wait for the crossing lights, etc. I knew that it was important to avoid cops, not to provoke them. Luckily there were only a couple of people in the store and one of them was a friend. She confirmed what I had seen in the mirror, that my pupils were of different sizes. One wasn't quite round.

I was fucked up.

I knew there was no way I could make any subjective decisions or know if I was correctly adhering to social customs. I didn't even know how to modulate my voice. Was this loud? Do I look like a regular person? Outside, my friend shivered so I asked her if it was cold because temperature-wise, for me, there was only tolerable/intolerable. (I found that out in the shower.) I guess I wasn't cold since I had no urge to change locations.

In no way was this like being drunk, even though I kept thinking I probably looked drunk. Although I still had control over my motor skills, I was very aware of my arms and legs. They seemed longer. Although walking was no problem, I felt more like I was loping. Objective observation of people under the influence of DM shows their gestures to be expansive and their strides to be longer than normal. So it wouldn't be fair to say that DM has no effect on motor skills. You can easily walk, but I doubt you could do ballet.

I understood that I was involved in a big contraption called civilization and that certain things were expected of me, but I could not comprehend what the hell they might be.

All the words that came out of my mouth seemed equal. Instead of saying "reduce it about 90 percent," I could have said "two eggs and some toast" and these two phrases would have been the same. The whole world was broken down into elemental parts, each being of equal value to the whole, which is to say, of no value at all.

I sat at a table and read a newspaper. It was the most absurd thing I had ever seen! Each story purported to be a description of a thing or event, or was supposed to convey "news" of reality in another place besides here. This seemed stupid. An article on the war that's going on in Burma was described as "the war the west forgot." It had an "at-a-glance" chart that said Burma had so many acres and was approximately three times the size of the state of Washington.

This was meaningless and I knew it. The story did not even begin to describe the tiniest fragment of the reality of what was happening in that place. Since I hadn't always been a reptile I knew things were what they call "complicated" and that the paper's pitiful attempt to categorize individuals as "rebels" or "insurgents" or to describe the reasons for the agony was ridiculous. (I laughed out loud.)

But back to being a reptile. I found it kind of pleasant. I was content to sit there and monitor my surroundings. I was alert, but not anxious.

If someone had come to me with an ax I would have acted appropriately. Fight or flight. Every now and then I would do a true "reality check" to make sure I wasn't masturbating or strangling someone, because of my vague awareness that more was expected of me than just being a reptile. At one point I ventured across the street to a take-out place to get something to eat. It was closed and yet there were workers inside. This truly confused me and I considered a way to simply run in, grab the food, and make off with some. Luckily, the take-out opened (it was now 6 A.M.) and I entered the front door like a normal customer.

It was mentally difficult to remember how to do a money-for-merchandise transaction and even more difficult to put it into words but I was successful. I ate bite by bite until I was full. If I had become full before finishing the hamburger, I think I would have simply let it fall from my hand.

> ## FREE ADVICE
> "Don't show your zine to your parents or employers, especially if you're living at home or using their machines to copy it."
>
> —Mark Maynard, *Crimewave U.S.A.*

The life of a reptile is boring to us, but I was never bored when I was a reptile. If something started to hurt me I took steps to get away from it; if it felt better over here, that's where I went. Now, twenty-four hours later, I'm beginning to get my neocortex back. Soon, I hope to be human again.

enlightenment

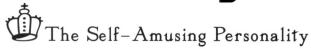 The Self-Amusing Personality

Candi Strecker launched **SIDNEY SUPPEY'S QUARTERLY & CONFUSED PET MONTHLY** *in 1979 to keep in touch with her college friends, all members of what she calls "the* Repo Man *generation." She didn't know the medium had a name so could only say, "Here's my . . . my . . . this thing I'm doing." The zine form "fits my personality," Candi says now. "I'm a bit shy, a bit of a perfectionist, a bit obsessed with reading and clipping tiny bits out of old and new magazines and trying to find connections among them." She recently published highlights from her first sixteen issues, including this 1982 selection. Candi calls it "one of the favorite things I've written, and more or less my personal credo."*

Let me ask you something. How do you respond to a beer-can hat?

This is not a laughing matter. And yes, I'm talking about those beer-can hats that are so popular on the flea market circuit, made by clipping the logo segments from beer cans and crocheting them together with cheap yarn to make a floppy-brimmed, preposterous hat.

I would like to think that I know a little something about you who are reading this publication, that it would not have come into your hands if you did not share with me a certain attitude towards the world, a world epitomized by the beer-can hat. This grotesque little object is a failure in its ostensible role as "head covering." But as a cultural artifact, it speaks volumes: it represents a mass culture that rewards denial of dignity, that fears idle time and promotes useless hobby-craft as a means to fill it, that supports mindless group beer-drinking, that encourages allegiance to brand names. It's a sorry representation of everything I loathe about the society I inhabit, and yet . . . and yet . . . I can't turn away. I look in fascination, and then I start to laugh, and then I almost want to cheer the endless inventiveness of a culture that fabricates such gadgets. Like a person who passes a squashed rat while walking along the highway, I cannot suppress the perverse urge to look.

Maybe for you it's not the beer-can hat. Maybe it's the dashboard waving-hand, or the jogging-shoe keychain ornament, or the lawn flamingo or the *National Enquirer*—you have your list, I have mine. The crucial thing is that we keep these mental lists, trading tales of our latest sightings with other connoisseurs. Something has made our vision of the world go a bit askew, and instead of accepting the satisfactions that derive from being players in our society, we create our own amusement by examining the output of that society. If you feel that unique mixed emotion of amused horror much of the time, you're probably what I've come to call a Self-Amusing Personality (SAP).

Most SAPs don't just stop at wry observation. Spotting a beer-can hat for the first time, they wonder: Where did it come from? Who invented it? How did the idea spread? What is a person thinking while wearing one? In how many years will it be thrown away? In working out the answers to such questions, one may see startling connections among the phenomena observed. This is self-amusement at its best. Just as a visual artist might observe how sunlight strikes an apple, and by painting it not only communicate his observation but irreversibly change how others see sunlit apples, a SAP makes fresh observations on human behavior within his or her culture. One might even go so far as to call truly astute SAPs "culture artists."

Often, a culture artist's insights are communicated to an audience of none, or one, being passed along in jokes, in offhand remarks, in letters, or in notebooks, for want of any better outlet. A few find a receptive audience, even make a living from their observations—George Carlin comes to mind, along with certain other comedians, writers, cartoonists, and satirists. But most SAPs only "moonlight" in their activities; they may not have the will or the talent to support themselves as writers or artists full-time. Yet they still have worthwhile observations, which they are driven to communicate.

For most SAPs, each new day brings the problem of communicating with non-SAPs, that vast majority of people who never begin a sentence "Did you ever notice that . . . ?" Inevitably, SAPs must seek other SAPs, and this search often leads one into fandoms, the subcultures of enthusiasts and collectors. Within a fandom, a SAP may have the pleasure and relief of meeting others like him/herself, others who have passions and theories. Among postcard collectors, one may find another who's amused by representations of flamingos; among comic-book fans, someone else who savors the good-badness of "The Flintstones." Thus SAPs meet SAPs and set up networks of SAPs within networks of fans.

This gratifying activity has its natural limits, of course. The odds of encountering SAPs within a fandom are better than the odds in the real world; that's precisely their attraction to SAPs. But just as in the real world, most fans are not SAPs (more likely, they're timid pack-rats).

Then there's the problem of crossing over from one context to another. I've met many self-amused friends through science-fiction fandom, but if I tried to bring a postcard-collecting SAP into that circle he or she would probably protest, "But I don't like science fiction." Fandoms have their pleasures and their purposes, but as long as each focuses on a single topic, the SAPs in each group are kept from realizing that they all share a common outlook. What if an organization could make contact with the SAPs in all the fandoms and pull them together into one big network? Once organized, would we look at our organization with amused horror?

Like A Hole in Your Head

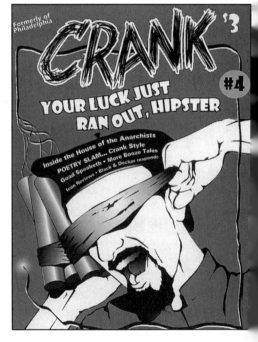

You wanna know what **CRANK** *is about? Check out the contents of the 1994 debut of Jeff Koyen's magazine of "poorly funded self-indulgence": 1. Fuck the Suburbs, 2. My Favorite Asshole, 3. The Lost Art of the Drunken Drive, 4. A Tip Sheet for New Stalkers, 5. My Friend AIDS. Jeff is the kind of crank who invites amateur poets (is there any other kind?) to send him their best stuff, then hands out awards like "Worst Line" or "Worst Overall Poet, Male." Mean-spirited, you say? Maybe* Crank *fodder such as "Anarchists: The Same Old Hippie Shit," "An Illustrated Guide to Converting Small Dead Mammals into Instruments of Destruction," or an excerpt from "The Crank Home Surgery Companion" is more your style. In this selection from his second issue, Jeff details the history and how-to of trepanation.**

* If you're dumb enough to try this, a hole in your head ain't gonna help.

The Greeks did it. The Romans did it. The Egyptians did it. Ancient Peruvians and the Neolithic French (as far back as ten thousand years ago) did it. What am I talking about? Trepanation, of course. In the strictest sense of the word, "to trepane" is nothing more than opening a hole in the skull, usually for medical purposes. But we're interested in more spirited experiments in skull digging.

In the Cuzco region of Peru, more than nine thousand trepanned skulls have been unearthed, many dating back to the first millennia before Christ. In the Paracas Indian site south of Lima, more than six percent of some ten thousand well-preserved bodies show evidence of trepanation. More recently, 120 prehistoric skulls were found across European archeological sites. Of these, forty had manmade cranial breaches. Injuries? Perhaps. But consider one skull discovered in the 1800s. The opening in this skull was unquestionably manmade, evidenced from the cross-hatched incisions.

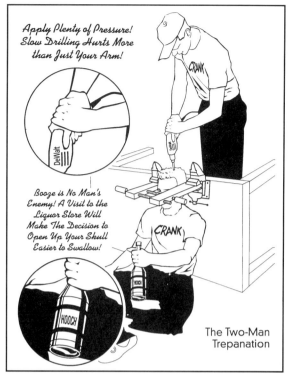

Apply Plenty of Pressure! Slow Drilling Hurts More than Just Your Arm!

Booze is No Man's Enemy! A Visit to the Liquor Store Will Make The Decision to Open Up Your Skull Easier to Swallow!

The Two-Man Trepanation

Illustration by Dennis McGee

In brief, it seems that *everybody was opening their fucking skulls.*

There are three theories as to why: 1) to treat depressed skull fractures (a medical procedure); 2) to treat headaches, convulsions, and mental disorders (in the Middle Ages, holes were drilled in skulls to let demons out); or 3) to endow special mental powers on anyone who survived the procedure. Ask Joey Mellen and Amanda Fielding about that last one. They're a couple in England who drilled holes in their heads and claim they have never been happier.

Modern trepanation can be traced to the Dutch doctor Bart Hughes, who in 1962 put forth a radical idea. As we age, our skulls slowly harden and this new nonelasticity thereby restricts the blood flow through our brains. Dr. Bart surmised that an individual can temporarily adjust this situation by a number of methods, such as jumping from a hot bath into a cold one, standing on your head, or the use of drugs. But he was looking for something more permanent. So one day he cut a small hole in his skull with an electric drill. He never felt better! Soon after, the good doctor was thrown in a mental hospital.

In 1965, Joey Mellen met Dr. Bart (then back in society) and decided to put a hole in his own head. One weekend he bought a manually operated trepan, hypodermic needles, a local anesthetic, and tabs of LSD. His friend Amanda agreed to help. The hole was coming along nicely when Joey collapsed. After a quick trip to the hospital and a stern warning from the doctors (instant death, etc.), Joey and Amanda returned to her home and the drilling was completed.

"After some time there was an ominous sounding schlurp and the sound of bubbling," Joey recalls in his autobiography, "Bore Hole." "I drew the trepan out and the gurgling continued. It sounded like air bubbles. I looked at the trepan and there was a bit of bone in it. At last! If only I had an electric drill it would have been so much simpler. I decided to call it a day. I bandaged up my head and cleared away the mess."

It took five more drilling sessions before Joey was satisfied, and then Amanda took her turn (she even filmed it). Today, according to news reports, the couple lives happily in Chelsea, has a child, owns an art gallery, and lectures on the benefits of trepanation.

If you're like me, the question you're asking yourself right now is "How? How can I drill a hole in my skull in the privacy and comfort of my own home?"

The Tools

I took a trip to a local hardware store in search of the right trepanation equipment at the right price. I followed three guidelines:

1. Buy only dependable hardware—having the drill crap out in the middle of the procedure could be a problem.

2. Try to save money—this ain't no suicide; you've still got to pay the rent, even with a hole in your head.

3. Buy American.

We'll assume that, like Joey, you have a friend who can help you trepan yourself. Here's the shopping list:

3 ½" Steel Beam Vice Bench ($69.99)
My head fit inside this model with half an inch to spare on either side. Perfect! With a couple of rags to protect your ears, your buddy will have a good angle and you won't be able to twitch or flinch when the hole gets started.

8" Steel C-Clamp ($12.49)
This clamp is listed only if the $69.99 vice bench is over your budget. I'm warning you, though—keeping your head still will be difficult. And who can't use a quality vice, anyway?

Tool Belt ($15.99)
Once your head is clamped down, you won't have much mobility. I would purchase a tool belt to keep the booze and first-aid supplies within easy reach.

Lifter's Belt ($34.99)
The last thing you want to do is throw your back out thrashing around. Consider it.

Professional Reversible Spade Handle 1/2" Drill ($156.99)
Sure, it's expensive. But this is the motherfucker of all drills. Two handles (one on the side, one at the rear). Triple gear reduction. 100% Ball and Roller Bearings. 7.0 amps. 450 rpm. Rear handle adjustable in 90° increments. Fairly lightweight. Reversible. With this baby in

hand, your friend will *enjoy* liberating your brain. MADE IN USA.

Again, if your budget doesn't allow for a two-handled beast, consider:

Black & Decker D1000 ⅜" Drill ($34.94)

Single speed, reversible, 2-year warranty, and (this is important) a lock-on button. When I asked Jim, the fellow working the hardware department, which drill he would use if he were drilling a hole in his head, he told me that "any of the Black & Decker's are top of the line—the D1000, though, is a real nice drill, and it's on sale." *Sold!*

So, you're all ready to drill. But wait—what kind of drill BIT are you going to use, smart guy? Standard wood/metal? Wood boring? Tile and ceramic? I asked Jim for his expert advice:

Me: "So what kind of bit should I use?"
Him: "I think you have to figure out which is best for what you're working on."
Me: "I'm the guy who's drilling the hole in his head. I was in yesterday. You recommended the Black & Decker D1000."
Him: "Oh, yeah, I remember you. That's a good drill."
Me: "So which kind of bit should I use? Wood boring?"
Him: "You definitely have to figure out which one is best for what you're working on. I don't know about that stuff."
Me: "This isn't trial and error, Jim. I'm drilling a hole in my head."
Him: "I don't know. Sorry."

I was on my own. How about . . .

Standard Wood/Metal Bits (⁷⁄₁₆", ¹⁵⁄₃₂" or ½")

These are the normal drill bits you'd use to put a hole in the wall. They're also the bits I assume most people would use to put a hole in their head. I am concerned that they will provide a slow start, but the larger bits seem too dangerous.

Assemble the First Aid

Whenever you open up any part of your body, something could go wrong. Trepanation is no exception.

Sterile Pads, 4"x4", Box of 25 ($7.99)

You're going to bleed, a lot. Get two boxes.

Witch Hazel, three quarts (@$1.87 each)

Close your eyes and pour it right on your head.

Cotton Roll ($4.99)

Wrap yourself up like The Mummy. It'll be fun.

Liquor (various)

Booze will play a major role in your decision to drill a hole in your head.

Anesthesia

The strongest over-the-counter topical anesthetic comes in products such as Anbesol and Chloraseptic.
You might as well buy a shitload and numb yourself beforehand. Look for the ingredient Benzocaine, or ask your pharmacist. Also, grab some Advil.

Iodine, Rubbing Alcohol, Neosporin

All of these things will help keep your new orifice clean.

Total Expense

So how much is this trip to enlightenment going to cost? By my calculations, about $317.52 (give or take your booze allotment). And don't forget film—no sense having to do it again for the camera.

eras

It's A Wonderful Lifestyle

A Seventies Flashback:
Part One

Panasonic •••• 8 TRACK PLAYER

$4.00

Why the Seventies?

Candi Strecker, who was fourteen when the seventies began, spent more than a year researching and writing **IT'S A WONDERFUL LIFESTYLE,** *her two-part zine history of the music, cars, clothes, hairstyles, television, and films of the decade. Remember unisex, bionic, gasohol, macramé, superstar, feather jewelry, L.E.D., crocheted neckties, sun tea, mug trees, bottle cutting, Earth Shoes, assertiveness training, and roller disco? Or that long before there were designer jeans, people checked sneaker stripes? Or "Don't hit my hair!" (Saturday Night Fever, 1977)? In this excerpt from her introduction, Candi explains why the seventies matter.*

From today's perspective, it's easy to see the seventies as a sort of cheeselike substrate, a non-nutritive filler between the higher-fiber LSD and MBA decades. But while that decade was happening, you had no way of knowing you were in the middle of something. What the era felt like was not transition, but emptiness. With no clear sense of direction, all we had to orient ourselves were the confusing Doppler-effect sounds of one trend-train going and another one coming.

Hate is a useful reaction to the present, because it helps you maintain your perspective on the world you're wading hip-deep in. But once an era slips into the past, you don't need the tool of hate in order to be objective about it. It can't bite you anymore: you're free to pick it up, probe it, play with it, examine it. It made sense to hate the seventies during the seventies. But it's a waste of energy to hate the seventies now.

Yet many people loudly insist they hated every minute of the Avocado Decade. It's hard to pin down why. If pressed, people will name a couple of fads or pop songs that were hideous indeed—but you could pull equally embarrassing examples out of the popular culture of any decade of this century. "Tie A Yellow Ribbon 'Round The Old Oak Tree" is a silly song, but no sillier than "Mairzy Doats" or "Funky Cold Medina." What was unique about the seventies was not its goofy fads but its obsession with "being hip." Blame it on baby boom demographics: the desire to be seen as hip or fashionable is a preoccupation of people in their teens and twenties, and there was a conspicuous bulge in the number of people in that age range during the seventies. The fads of the seventies were no stupider than those of any other decade, but there were more of them.

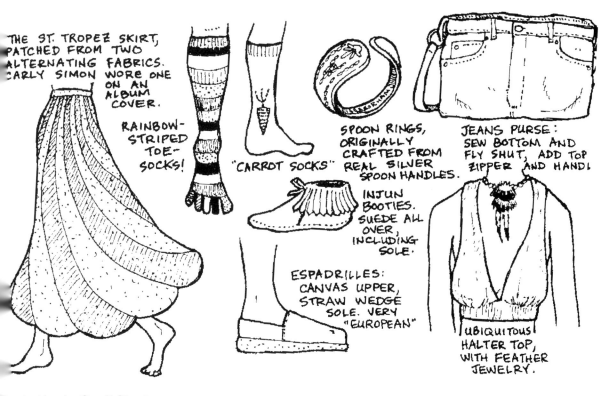

THE ST. TROPEZ SKIRT, PATCHED FROM TWO ALTERNATING FABRICS. CARLY SIMON WORE ONE ON AN ALBUM COVER.

RAINBOW-STRIPED TOE-SOCKS!

"CARROT SOCKS"

SPOON RINGS, ORIGINALLY CRAFTED FROM REAL SILVER SPOON HANDLES.

INJUN BOOTIES. SUEDE ALL OVER, INCLUDING SOLE.

ESPADRILLES: CANVAS UPPER, STRAW WEDGE SOLE. VERY "EUROPEAN"

JEANS PURSE: SEW BOTTOM AND FLY SHUT, ADD TOP ZIPPER AND HANDL

UBIQUITOUS HALTER TOP, WITH FEATHER JEWELRY.

ustration by Candi Strecker

Life in an era of rapid fad cycles can be frustrating and unsettling; it can make even the heppest person begin each morning feeling a bit obsolete. If the seventies was a decade of more fads and fashions than ever before, it was correspondingly a decade of more failures to be hip and fashionable. No wonder so many people look back at the seventies as their personal "gauche" decade, a time when they tried hard but often failed. This may explain why people try so hard to disassociate themselves from the era. They not only want to pretend they didn't participate in it, but even go so far as to pretend they weren't there at all. The seventies' fads aren't what embarrass us; it's the knowledge that we once took them seriously.

The upshot is that our society practices mass denial about an entire decade of its recent history. I hesitate to draw such an extreme parallel, but like Germans after World War II who claim they never joined the Nazi party, people today won't admit they ever did "The Hustle" or studied CB slang or made macramé plant-slings. And the more we deny the seventies, the more the decade haunts and troubles us. We treat this part of our past like a disease in remission; we dread that the seventies lies dormant within us, and might flare up again at any time. Our pursuit of hipness in the present must be justified by mocking our pursuit of it in the past. But mocking one's past won't break the deadly cycle of hipness.

The only cure, the therapy our society needs, is to face our fears and insecurities and learn to laugh at ourselves—not clammy nervous laughter, but cleansing, forgiving laughter. We need to laugh at our old platform shoes but simultaneously know we're no wiser today in our new Nike pump-ups.

We'd all like to pretend otherwise, but unless you're Karen Ann Quinlan and spent the decade in a coma, *you don't have any excuse for the seventies.* You were there, you did participate in it, you were a collaborator. It's time to stop repressing our memories of the seventies, and gently open the doors on our cultural amnesia about the decade. Set the Wayback for 1970, put on that Yes album you haven't played since college, settle down in the beanbag chair, and immerse yourself in these repressed memories. My guess is that, as the bits and pieces of the decade wash over you, you'll feel not revulsion but a strange sense of relief—and soon, genuine interest. The seventies may be characterized by more blundering than purposeful achievement, by fads consumed and discarded at the speed of light, by contradiction instead of consistency—but that's exactly what makes the decade rich and fascinating.

I'm on "Geraldo!"

Mark Maynard and Linette Lao were watching the tube one day in 1994 when an announcer blared, "CRIMEWAVE U.S.A.! Next on 'Inside Edition.'" It seemed like a great name for a zine, so it became one. Linette had just landed a job with access to scanners, cameras, and office supplies; when Mark was hired as a copy shop manager, they became the perfect zine couple. In this selection from issue 4, Mark recounts his first and only appearance as an audience member on "Geraldo!"

After we waited for a long time, Geraldo finally introduced the show. It was called "Strange and Twisted Affairs."

We met a woman from West Virginia who called her ex-boyfriend's new, much older girlfriend a "child-molesting bitch." In response, the ex-boyfriend told her that he never loved her, and that she was just "an easy piece." I was lucky enough to be sitting right in front of them. That's my head blocking his left leg from your view.

Geraldo told us about the next guest, a guy named Rob. He asked us to treat him gently because he'd recently tried to kill himself after catching his wife having sex with his dad. Geraldo appeared truly concerned. Later, on TV, I saw that the caption under Rob's face said, "Rob—Can't Satisfy Wife." Maybe Geraldo forgot.

Then we met twin brothers. The one on the left was pissed at the one on the right, who stole his girlfriend while he was away fishing in northern Michigan. The brother who stole the girlfriend said his twin deserved to have her stolen from him because he was cheating, not fishing, on his trip up north. He even had evidence. Apparently, "dude didn't even take a pole."

I was determined to be on TV and have Geraldo touch me (just check out that look of demented intent on my face), so I raised my hand during the commercial break when they asked if any of us had questions. I told one of Geraldo's lovely assistants that I wanted to ask something I really had no intention of asking. She liked the idea a lot and told Geraldo to talk to me first.

I began to think of a new and better question as soon as she left me. (This is my sly look.) It had to be something clever and funny and dirty, too. There had to be something for everyone. I wanted to be as outrageous as I could without being either escorted from the building or edited out of the show.

After the commercial, Geraldo pulled me up from my seat and said, "Welcome back everyone. We've calmed things here in the studio temporarily." Then he turned to me and said, "Yes, sir." I waved at everyone on the stage (for what reason I have no idea) and then leveled my hand and stuck out my index finger toward the twin who had lost his love. "Yeah, this is for Jamie," I said. "I've read things before about twins where like, if one gets hit in the thumb with a hammer, the other can feel it . . ."

"I was wondering if you had any idea that she (here I pivoted to point at his ex-girlfriend) was going down on your brother when you were up north? Do you recall feeling anything unusual and yet familiar?"

After a moment of contemplative silence, the crowd erupted in applause and laughter. The brother that got gone down on said, "It wasn't like that. It wasn't like that." I still can't figure out what the hell he meant. I guess he meant that he didn't knowingly send a telepathic boner to his twin. Neither brother looked too amused. I started to get scared.

Not wanting to relinquish the spotlight, I went on to mumble, "And also, I just think that this woman here is disgusting!" pointing to one of the disgusting women on stage. Geraldo said, "Alright, alright . . ." and pushed me back into my seat.

The crowd was still laughing as Geraldo pointed down at me and said . . . "I caution you, they are both super-middleweights!"

fashion

A Day in the Life of Matt's Hair

ECDYSIS: **Matt Wolka's Journal of Domestic Life** *said hello in 1993 with a lament about the boneheads who moved his piano from Staten Island to Chicago. The issue closed with his wife Mary Kay's ingenious "fell asleep/didn't fall asleep" film reviews. (She took these photos of Matt's hair.) For subsequent issues, Matt snapped shots of empty bikinis, created a mathematical formula for traffic jams, assigned a friend to test-drive the Wonderbra, and devoted a special edition to the elusive yak (including a review of yak steak and an unrelated trip to Yaak, Montana). Matt also knows lots of word games and puzzles.*

7:58 am

4:46 pm

10:53 pm

12:18 pm

8:13 am

8:23 am

8:16 am

▽ Fruitleather Underwear

Retro Hell (part one) / Issue #25   U.S.A. $3.95 / Canada $5.50

You may know Darby Romeo from The I Hate Brenda Newsletter, *her one-shot zine that dissed Brenda Walsh of "Beverly Hills 90210." But that was just a fling.* **BEN IS DEAD** *(named for an ex-boyfriend) is Darby's long-term relationship. She began the zine on Halloween in 1988 as "a point to move from" and has since published nearly thirty issues covering topics such as grossness, glamour, death, censorship, revenge, obsessions, and retro culture. Says Will Pfeifer of* Underbelly: *"Ben Is Dead embodies the great zine ideal of examining a subject—any subject—until it's completely, utterly exhausted." In this selection from the sold-out sex issue, Cliff Thurber shares an old family recipe.*

Well folks, contrary to White House reports, we're still in the depths of an interminable recession. Therefore, resourcefulness is the operative word. In my travels and research for the sex issue, I've come to one definitive conclusion: there is price gouging going on in the nation's sex shops. The price of edible panties has gone up 50 percent. A year and a half ago, a pair could be purchased for $5. The current price is $7.50. As you know, *Ben Is Dead* is always looking out for your best interests (see the broke issue). I tracked down the world-renowned pastry chef Brendt Rogers of Campanile Restaurant only to find his novelty can be prepared in relatively little time in your own kitchen. Here's the deal:

BASIC INGREDIENTS:

3 large bananas
1 1/4 cups of sugar
(concentrated fruit juices can be substituted, use half the amount)
1 tablespoon lemon juice
1 tablespoon oil

Step 1 : Preheat oven to 200° Fahrenheit.
Step 2 : Lightly oil parchment paper (wax paper) and cut paper to size of pan (12" x 18").
Step 3 : Puree bananas in a Cuisinart until completely smooth. With spatula, remove puree, place in bowl, then add sugar and lemon juice and mix until incorporated.

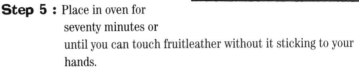

Step 4 : Pour banana mix on tray, then spread evenly over length of pan(s) with bent dick spatula.

Step 5 : Place in oven for seventy minutes or until you can touch fruitleather without it sticking to your hands.

Step 6 : Remove and let cool.

Step 7 : Lightly peel fruitleather from corner in one complete swath.

Step 8 : Sneak a pair of recipient's underwear as a template for cut line. Lay front side down and trace outline, leaving a narrow strip for the crotch. Repeat for back side, leaving a crotchpiece as well. This is important as the crotch piece must be doubled because female juices will break down the leather.

Step 9 : Putting both sides together is done simply by licking the seams and overlapping a bit (1/4 to 1/2 inch). Do the same overlap and licking procedures with crotch pieces. The excess fruitleather has sundry uses such as lick and stick pasties or Mexican penal serapes.

Enjoy!

Photos by Scott Sener

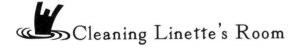

games

Cleaning Linette's Room

During a visit home in the summer of 1995, Linette Lao decided it was time to organize the stuff piled in her childhood room. "My friend Cristina, who drew this cartoon, was saying you don't need that or I'll take that," says Linette, coeditor of **CRIMEWAVE U.S.A.** *"I need someone like that around all the time—a director of throwing things away."*

CLEANING LINETTE'S ROOM!

Guess where each
object belongs according
to our eclectic heroine...

By C.M.
Di Chiera
1/96

① scuzzey styra-foam

② a plastic banana

③ Barbie in a jar with a faucet

④ broken ceramic fruit sculpture

⑤ Plastic, fake CB Thing

⑥ colorful Fashion wire wire

⑦ one white boot

⑧ a list
50 People
with the
name Billy
1. Billy the Kid
2. Billy Graham
3. Billie Holiday
4. Billy Jean King
5. Billy Joel
6. Billy RueCirne
7. Billy Clinton

⑨ astro-turf thing place mat

Your Choices Are:

A. Give Away—
"Somebody could use this,
couldn't they?"

B. Throw Away—
"Do You Want
this?"

C. Keep—
"Just put it
over there"

And Now For the Exciting Conclusion of CLEANING LINETTE'S ROOM!

By C.M. DiChiera
1/96

① keep— "That's my cheese costume!"

② keep— "That's part of my fake fruit collection!"

③ keep— "I made that in my 3-D Design class. Oh, yeah, you were in that class! I opened that jar up about a month ago & it has developed the most horrible smell! I never would have guessed that barbie was capable of producing such a disgusting smell. It was like I hit a wall of stink! Oh, I have to keep that!"

④ keep— "That's part of my fake fruit collection too. I just have to find the piece that broke off & glue it back."

⑤ keep— "That's my C.B. Bank!"

⑥ keep— "Umm... I forgot why I bought that. I'll use it for something."

⑦ keep— "My go-go boots! They're 2 sizes too small. But the other one's around here somewhere!"

⑧ keep— "Oh, there's another list around here some place with the name Vinnie. I have to keep that. They're like a set!"

⑨ keep— "I made that in my 3-D Design class. Oh, yeah, I met you in that class. Remember my astro-turf project? I've gotta keep that!"

~ If you answered c-keep for all, you win!! ~

👄 Hide-and-Seek

Nancy Bonnell-Kangas has a great sense of humor, and of the absurd, and she can draw. What more do you need? **NANCY'S MAGAZINE,** *which debuted in 1983, is a fresh face on the zine horizon, filled with whimsical cartoons, quizzes, unscientific polls, recipes, and essays. Her classic ground issue included a free seed packet, a guide to whether you should invest in the crepe sole business, Shakespearean references to mud, facts about concrete, and a survey of her friends about soil's effect on human behavior. Even after all that, says Nancy, "the world is bursting with pockets of as-yet unexaminedness." Nancy's brother, Tom Kangas, wrote this essay for her youth issue.*

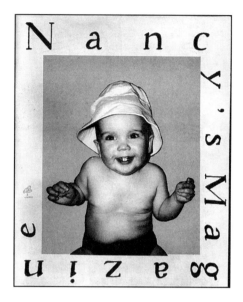

To play together we made rules. Hide-and-seek was about running away and finding a very small place you could fit into. You giggled and stifled it because you realized there was silence. You listened more intently than ever! Waiting to be discovered or surprised. At last you became bored. The game began to play on you . . . this was a real game, wasn't it? They didn't run away to play another game? The game they really wanted to play? To play without me? . . . Lost in these thoughts, it was almost a letdown when "it" turned the corner and there you were together.

Being it was another world. It was thrust upon you. There was the counting. The first thing you had to do. Count so many numbers. Aloud, louder! You wanted to say the numbers faster. Because they were getting away, because they had time to really hide themselves, because you would never find them.

You figure that maybe one or two would be simple to find, the others probably harder. But it is later. The game has been played more than once. The good places and the obvious spots have been abandoned. This you discover—one by one. Your tactics are silence and a keen eye.

The silence begins to get to you. This game you are playing, it toys with you, whispers in your ear, lets you in on a secret, telling you . . . this wasn't a real game. They ran away to play another. The game they really wanted to play. Without you.

The night is cooler now. Everything is a little cruel. Looking about you, you don't have the others; you have the cruel night. You are tired.

ZINE VOICES

"As a college freshman I received a visit from Art Garfunkel; he'd lived in the same dorm room as a student. So I started *Art for Art's Sake,* a newsletter that was purportedly the house organ of the Garfunkel museum but actually was a vehicle for distributing inane material. After I graduated, I got my hands on *The Realist* and *Army Man,* the legendary funzine that 'Simpsons' writer George Meyer put out to kill time during the writers' strike. I thought that this should be my calling."

—Don Steinberg, *Meanwhile . . .*

Two Minutes' Batchat with Adam West

Zine editors take what they can get when it comes to interviewing celebrities. After being denied a sit-down with the star of TV's "Batman" series, **HITCH** *editor Rod Lott cornered his childhood hero during a publicity stop at a local supermarket. The interview took place as West signed Rod's "Batman" video.*

Hitch: Have you read Burt Ward's* book yet?
West: I scanned it.
Hitch: So what did you think?
West: Trashy. Unbelievably trashy. He made me out to be like Errol Flynn's trainer . . . Poor Burt.
Hitch: So what did you think of "Batman Forever"?
West: I saw it on an airplane recently, and I liked it better than the first two films.
Hitch: Why?
West: I thought it was much more spirited and lighthearted.
Hitch: Did you ever get chafed sliding down the Batpole?
West: No, but it had wet paint on it sometimes.

* Burt Ward played Robin

Jail Break! from MOO juice

hunks

Their World of Love

Inspired in part by Ivan Stang's classic guidebook, High Weirdness by Mail, *Dan Kelly launched his first zine in 1991 with the help of friends Kathy Moseley and Darrin Sullivan. Their latest creation is* **CHUM**, *which has detailed the history of cinema sluts, how to be a film snob, and the essential elements of cocktail culture. Hunk lover Leslie Stella contributed this selection for issue 3. "If I could be a girl," says Dan, "I would want to be Leslie— only with a Gucci wardrobe and a tony red sportscar."*

I recently had the indistinct pleasure of interviewing two of the world's most adored men: Yanni, Greek musical stylist, and Fabio, Italian subject of photos and illustrations and fake butter spokesman. Please enjoy them, as I have.

What is the difference between Yanni and Fabio?

F: It is obvious, is it not? My hair is kissed by the sun, streaked with gold, the same color of the beach near my villa in Italy. It is this same beach where I would crawl out of the waves on my belly to come get you.

Y: My tresses are black as midnight, the same color as the night sky over the Acropolis when I played my wonderful concert and made my mother cry.

F: Also, I am a very masculine man. I like to wear the chest-revealing shirts. My chest—or my breasts, as I like to call them—is a very big chest. I lift the weights to increase the size. A woman likes to see that I can carry her over the beach, or over some rocks if they are in the way.

Y: I give the ladies strength through my music to carry themselves.

Do you feel that your audiences cross over at all? Do you have the same fans?

Y: Me, I would say no. A person must love sweet music first in order to love me, even though my wavy hair and large mustache are tempting. A fan of Fabio is primarily interested in his breasts.

F: That is typical, coming from a Greek. The women may love my body, my hair, my strength and smell. But they love most that I am able to bring out their most womanly qualities. My fans are not interested in silly electronic orchestras. They want the reality of a man enfolding his powerful arms around their tender bodies.

What was the most important event in your career?

F: My fragrance contract. You have seen the pictures in the magazines, no doubt. I am naked and am crawling out of the Mediterranean on my belly to come get you.

Y: Again, I refer back to my concert at the Acropolis. I wept during one particularly moving piece of mine. Also to know that my mother sat weeping in the audience next to my lady love, Linda Evans, this made me feel so special inside.

How do you respond to the accusation people have made about your work being fluffy and shallow?
Y: What people? Who is saying this?
F: I am sure I do not know what you mean. I am Fabio. I pose for romantic book covers, I am in the magazines, I give pleasure. No one has complained.

Why just one name?
Y: My last name is too hard for the ladies to pronounce. Let them know that I will always be their Yanni. No more, no less.
F: It is more romantic, no? "Fabio . . ." It just sounds more sexual. You do not say, "Mr. Tiger" or "Sir Lion of the Forest." You just say "tiger" or "lion." Growling like a savage animal—"tiger!" "Fabio!"

Is there any love on the horizon for Fabio?
F: Only one woman for me? Look at me! Fabio is made for pleasure-giving. I want to enjoy many women, and to let them enjoy me. But when a woman is with me, for that short time she is my woman. She feels the specialness, the pleasure, of me and my woman pleasure-giving, my special sensualness and . . . uh . . . our sensual pleasure-making.
Y: I give Linda Evans plenty of pleasure.

Do you see any plans for a collaboration between Yanni and Fabio? Perhaps a Fabio workout video set to Yanni's music?
Y: I am afraid I do not see this happening. Yanni's ladies would feel sick at the sight of Fabio's vulgar twitching set to my beautiful music.
F: I must agree. Fabio's women could not bear the offense of watching my strongness be encompassed by Yanni's girlish piano tinklings.

Thank you both.

ZINE VOICES

"I publish because I don't know anything else. I grew up with it, and I don't know how you stay sane without some kind of creative outlet and connection with other people."
—Aaron Cometbus, *Cometbus*

jokers

The Laugh Makers

XYY comes from the criminal chromosome theory that was a popular homicide defense tactic in the 1950s," explains John F. Kelly, its creator. "As the theory went, men with an extra Y chromosome were more prone to violence. The zine has evolved into a sort of demented kids' magazine, featuring comics, a fascination with science and medicine, and articles about tough guys. One reviewer called it 'Boy's Life for drunken mutants,' and I think that's as good a description as any." This interview, conducted by John and Mark Newgarden, appeared in issue 4.*

Recently we traveled to Neptune, New Jersey, to speak with seventy-six-year-old Bud Adams, owner of the S.S. Adams Company, "the world's largest manufacturer of practical jokes and magic tricks." The son of Sam Adams (the self-proclaimed inventor of the Joy Buzzer), he told us about his many years of providing merriment to the masses. He also led us on a guided tour of the factory, pointing with pride to happy workers producing Snake in the Cans, Squirt Nickels, and Magic Wands. What follows is a candid conversation with one of the people who make us laugh:

XYY: When did your father start the company?

Adams: 1906. He started it in Plainfield, New Jersey, and then he moved it to Asbury Park in the early twenties. Then we moved to this building in 1933 or '34.

XYY: What were the first products he sold?

Adams: The first was Sneezing Powder. My father got into that by accident. He was a salesman for a coal tar company and they extracted various materials from the coal tar, one of which made everyone sneeze. So he got it, put it into little packages, and sold it to his friends for a nickel or a dime. Then business started getting good. So he rented a room in Plainfield, and he had a girl working at a card table putting Sneezing Powder into envelopes all day long. From there he went into a rather nasty line of jokes. He made Itching Powder, Stink Bombs, and he also made up one item which we still sell, the Dribble Glass.

XYY: So you no longer sell Itching Powder.

Adams: Oh, no. We wouldn't dare. Itching Powder has put people into the hospital. Sneezing Powder contains something that is very injurious. But it's funny as the devil. If I wanted to make someone sneeze, I'd put this little package against the key hole of the door and fill the room with Sneezing Powder, and it worked. It really worked.

XYY: Someone's still selling it. I was in a novelty store and they had it. It looked like it was imported. It had German writing on it.

Adams: Sneezing Powder? No, today it's made with a type of pepper. Itching Powder is still imported. It's made from a weed that grows in India. If any cattle get into the weed, they have to be destroyed.

XYY: They can't stop scratching themselves?

Adams: Oh, they just go crazy.

XYY: What other products did your father make?

Adams: He made a can, it looked like a plain raspberry jam can, and if you opened it, a spring cloth-covered snake jumped out.

XYY: How did the Joy Buzzer come about?

Adams: My father went to Germany in 1928 and he met a clever Jewish tool and dye maker, who showed him an early, rather large version of the Buzzer. My father told him to make it small, which he did. It was four inches in diameter and

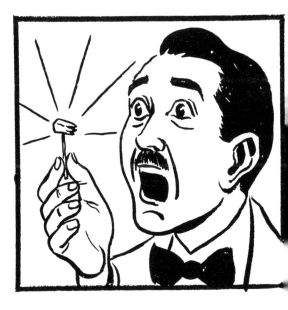

one inch thick. But then Hitler came into power, and the Jews were persecuted. So my father got a letter from the tool maker that said that for a small amount of money he would sell him the tools he used to make the Joy Buzzers. My father sent him the check and that was the last we heard of him. I certainly hope that he got out of Germany. That must have been his travel money.

I've worked all my life to improve the buzzer. I cut out a lot of the manufacturing process—I didn't cheapen it. I made it better. Today it's a relatively minor job. We throw a lot of parts together and we hit it once and it's finished.

XYY: How does the Joy Buzzer work?

Adams (giving us a quizzical look): You wind it up, shake hands with somebody and they get a buzz. If you sit on it, you get a surprise (laughter).

XYY: Has the buzz changed over the years?

Adams: Oh, yes. Today it's much stronger.

XYY: Do you think people today need a stronger charge?

Adams: (No reply)

XYY: Um . . . did your father try out the products on his friends?

Adams: Yes, every one of them.

XYY: Was he a funny guy?

Adams: No, they called him "Silent Sam." He was rather sneaky. He was always pulling jokes.

XYY: What are some of the other early items that have lasted?

Adams: Most of them have been discontinued because of the labor required. But there's a Rubber Pencil that was made years ago and it used to retail for ten cents each. Now we make it a little better and it retails for $1.49. We also made a Shiner. You look through a tube and you get a black eye. We still make that. The Shooting Fountain Pen we still make.

XYY: What are some of the products that he made that just bombed, that never went anywhere?

Adams: Oh, he had lots of them—and I've had plenty myself. One day on the Fourth of July somebody was lighting a big firecracker in the middle of the street and I took a little bitty firecracker and I threw it under him. He jumped straight into the air. That led to an item that I made, a firecracker about an inch-and-a-quarter in diameter and six inches high. Under the firecracker was a bingo mechanism. So you would light the fuse and nothing would happen and then somebody would go over and pick up the firecracker and it would go bang.

XYY: How about the Whoopee Cushion?

Adams: Oh, that was a terrific item. Somebody came in to see my father to sell the idea—the original inventor. That must have been in the late thirties or early forties. My father turned it down and said, "That will never sell" (laughter).

XYY: How does Disappearing Ink work?

Adams: It's made with a very close pH factor. The difference between being acid and alkaloid is the difference between being visible or invisible, like water. And when that changes, due to absorption of carbon dioxide, then the color disappears.

XYY: Have competitors ever stolen your ideas?

Adams: All the time! The Hindu Cones [a magic trick] was knocked off in the Orient and it was very faithfully duplicated. They even put our patent number on it, and our names too (laughter).

XYY: Are most of your new items magic tricks rather than practical jokes?

Adams: Right now magic is easier to create.

XYY: It seems that you've done a rubber version of just about everything.

Adams: Oh, thumb tacks, coat hangers—you hang your coat on it and it falls off.

XYY: Did you ever carry X-Ray Specs?

Adams: No. We had an X-Ray Tube, though. You see the bones in your hand. That was a big seller. There was a little piece of a feather pasted over a tiny hole—if you looked at your hand, you'd see the outline and you'd see another darker area that looked like bones. They were Guinea Hen feathers.

XYY: What about exploding or sparkling matches?

Adams: We had them but they were dangerous. We used to have book matches, paper matches, and there was a little piece of fulminate on each match. My father and I bumped heads on that one. You'd light a match and it would whoosh up in your face.

XYY: When you were a kid, did you always have all the latest novelties to show off to your friends?

Adams: No, my father hung on to the samples.

XYY (pointing to item in an old Adams catalog): What about these? "Hitler Horse Cards?" "Strike a match on the horse's ass . . ."

Adams: Oh, that was funny! And it says, "Heil Hitler!" The message was written with invisible ink. If you struck a match on it, the heat would make the message show up. That was a scream.

XYY: How far back does Fake Dog Doo go?

Adams (suddenly irritated): I don't know. How far back do dogs go? When was the first dog invented?

XYY (nervously): Has that always been a big seller?

Adams: Always, yes.

Some Things I've Discovered about Clowns

It's difficult to believe that the eighty or so pages of illustrations clipped from old magazines, antique children's books, and out-of-date catalogs that make up **CRAP HOUND** *could be so mesmerizing. Maybe it's the weighty themes such as sex, death, and utensils around which Sean Tejaratchi arranges his discoveries. The most popular of Sean's "picture books for discussion and activity" was filled with scandalous sexual tidbits and kitchen gadgets; the following selection is taken from a more recent issue devoted to devils, fishing bait, and clowns.*

★ SOME THINGS I'VE DISCOVERED ABOUT CLOWNS ★

THE DISCOVERY

I discovered it halfway through the assembly of this issue, while reading *Brewer's Dictionary of Phrase and Fable*. It opened my eyes to the evil secret that lurks behind the powdered face of clowning. Children already know it, and I should have realized it long ago.

"**THE CLOWN OF CIRCUS AND PANTOMIME, IN HIS BAGGY COSTUME, WHITENED FACE, GROTESQUE RED LIPS, AND ODD LITTLE TUFT OF BLACK HAIR, IS PROBABLY A RELIC OF THE DEVIL, AS HE APPEARED IN MEDIEVAL MIRACLE PLAYS."**

A friend pointed out that I must have been subconsciously aware of all this when I chose the topics. He's probably right. It's too perfect to have been a coincidence. The Clown and the Devil are archetypes. From Tarot cards all the way up to the Batman and Joker, they're taking up space in our minds whether we want them there or not.

IT'S ALL A BIG LIE

In all fairness, I should admit I've always hated clowns. You probably hate clowns, too. Everything on earth with a brain larger than a walnut hates clowns. I think people *used to* really like them, but they've died off over the years, like those who witnessed the Civil War. The last living clown enthusiast died last year, leaving the clowns themselves as their own biggest fans. No doubt they've been waiting for this. Finally they can perpetuate the myth of their own popularity without interference.

The popularity of clowns seems to operate like an urban legend. "Everyone loves clowns?" Bullshit. Total clown propaganda. Where are all these people? It's always someone else's grandmother, or their ex-girlfriend's cousin who loves them. During the six month creation of this issue, *not a single person* expressed to me a positive opinion of clowns. Children, the clown's so-called "best friends," hate and fear them with an unrivaled passion. Of all the feelings a clown can provoke, joy seems to be right down near the bottom of the list, probably next to "thirst." Someone should tell these fuckers that a deathly white mask and exaggerated, blood red features are not the express route to a child's heart.

LAUGH WITH THEM, NOT AT THEM, YOU LITTLE FUCK

God forbid you suggest any of this to a clown. Clowns, you should realize, don't take kindly to any sort of criticism. I've been looking through issues of *Calliope* and *Clowning Around*, two of the trade journals of your savvy professional clown. The issues I had came out about two years after *Shakes the Clown*, and the publishers were still complaining bitterly. They recount the scenes, savoring each detail as a separate insult. Clowns see themselves as joyful embodiments of mirth and innocence, and anyone who says differently is smart-alec son of a bitch intent on shitting all over the tradition of goodwill and laughter clowns have worked so hard to maintain...*bitch bitch bitch* clownbashing *bitch bitch bitch* anti-clown agenda... That's another thing– they whine a lot.

Elsewhere, in the clown advice columns ("Dear Aunt Clowny"), the debate rages over when it's finally okay to cozy up to a good stiff drink. Can a clown be in costume when he hits the sauce? How about when he's performing at a bar? Moral dilemmas like these get a lot of space. Will insurance cover me in the event some kid chokes on my flaccid balloon animal? It confirmed a lot of my childhood fears to hear clowns policing themselves.

A SORDID PAST...

While laughter has always been central to clowning, it's important to remember that brutality and death have always been right there alongside it. Clowns have been tidied up like fairy tales, the blood scrubbed away and a happy face glued crookedly on. Themes of decapitation, dismemberment, and random violence were extremely common, and still are just below the surface. A famous skit features a clown barbershop, into which a terrified clown customer is dragged and held down as several huge, nicked, straight razors are produced. And what child doesn't squeal with delight when an argument between two clowns rapidly escalates into a full-fledged riot once the clown cop and his friendly nightstick arrive? It's just like real life! The traditional Punch and Judy show revolves around beatings and murder, including a wacky infanticide. Bloodshed– it's clowntastic!

A FEEBLE EXCUSE...

Clowns are quick to justify their existence with tales of countless visits to swollen children in hospitals all over the country. Even that fucker Ronald McDonald, very probably the most evil clown in history, operates a children's hospice. Well, it figures. I'm sure being terminally ill might take some of the edge off an encounter with a clown. If I were facing a horrible, wasting death every day, I might even be able to look a clown in the face and *smile*. Anyway, it's not as if these kids are going to leap up and run away. They're a captive audience, for Christ's sake. In fact, I'd like to present the theory that the entire Shriner Hospital organization exists to furnish clowns with a revolving audience of sick and dying kids. Remember, Clown Directive No. 7 *clearly states* a clown must perform in as many shows as he possibly can.

...AND THE GREAT SHRINER THREAT

Speaking of Shriners, pay close attention... this is where it gets confusing and weird. Jack Chick, creator of those small Christian comic book tracts and noted world historian, fingers the Masons (if you catch my drift) as Devil worshippers, despite their lip-service to Christian ideals. The red fez, Jack claims, commemorates the slaughter of a townful of Christians. The Masons' little toadies in the Devil's work are the Shriners, those fez-loving, community-oriented American businessmen. The Shriners, as you may recall, have built an immense circus empire, stocked with National Guard-like "Clown Units," activated in times of impending circus. To counter this admittedly demonic scheme, Christian churches have put their thinking caps on and come up with the fantastically bright idea of... that's right! Christian Clowns! Contingents of ministers, presumably unaware of the clown's wonderfully rich history and origins, done up in facepaint and loose clothing, handing out red love balloons, fondling trusting children, and spreading the Word to anyone who'll stop running long enough to listen. Devil worshippers pretending to be Christians disguising themselves as devils who've gradually disguised themselves as clowns so they can do evil versus Christians pretending to be devils who've gradually disguised themselves as clowns in the name of good. Thank God the conspiracy has been exposed. Sleep tight.

DANGER!

Finally, a word of caution. There seems to be a deliberate campaign to indoctrinate children into the "wholesome" world of the clown. Ronald McDonald (™) seems particularly eager to edge out the more traditional choice of Jesus Christ in the *"Bestest, Most Secretest Friend In The Whole Wide World"* sweepstakes. Never forget: a clown is an adult, most likely a man, who likes nothing better than to disguise his face and shoot the shit with preadolescent children. Clowns are not on a first name basis with reality. I've met a few clowns out of makeup, and they set off mental alarms all over the place. There seems to be a lot of clowns in Portland. I've seen them exiting the Burnside Bridge in beat up sedans, tires squealing as they round the corner. Maybe a member (if you catch my drift again) of the Portland Chapter of the Kooky Klown Klub will find this issue and write to complain. Oh well. Clowns are fuckers and perverts and I take nothing back. Come on, clowns! Come on, you pussies!

kooks

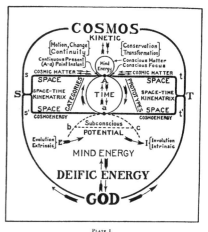

Inside the Kooks Archive

Donna Kossy loves kooks. Kooks love her. She gives their kooky theories a forum, and their kooky theories give her a voice. "If I just read enough kook material, I might be able to solve the mystery of the kooks," she says. "What makes them tick? Why do they believe what they believe? What are the kook types and traditions?" Yet even Donna has her limits: Kooks, but no cranks. "The difference between a kook and a crank is a lot like the difference between looking through a kaleidoscope and looking through somebody's thick eyeglasses: both of them impair your vision but one is a lot of fun and the other gives you a headache." For the third issue of **KOOKS***, Donna interviewed the curator of the little known Archives of Useless Research.*

Hidden within the university archives in Building Four at the Massachusetts Institute of Technology lie six boxes which hold the secrets of the universe. You'd expect such mysteries to be guarded by physics students armed with deadly orgone radiation weapons. But as every adept knows, the most important secrets are not secrets at all—they are available to anybody who cares enough to look for them.

Upon my first visit to the archives, I was overwhelmed by its sheer density. Each book, tract, or paper seemed to be the most amazing thing I'd ever seen. A spiral-bound illustrated text with "GOD'S TOYS—THE ATOMS" stamped on almost every page. A hardbound tome by George F. Gillette called "ORTHOD OXEN OF SCIENCE." A pamphlet proclaiming on its cover, "LO and BEHOLD! A Duplicate Key that Unlocks and Unmasks Mathematics!" with a supposed squaring of a circle inside (it's complicated). A 1935 treatise, "The Riddle of the Universe SOLVED to the Student Competents of my Race." Diagram after diagram showing all of creation on one page. A poster-sized explication of "124 Discoveries Made Between 1892 and 1930 by Seabury Doane Brewer, of Lake George, New York, and Montclair, New Jersey." Among his discoveries: "That temperature, with its variations, is one of the most wonderful things, and is always present everywhere," and "That physicians should be compelled to destroy all unfit specimens of humanity immediately upon their birth."

THE THEOCOSMIC DIAGRAM

Many of these items are date stamped Oct. 7, 1940. This is the date that Albert Ingalls, an editor at *Scientific American,* made his contribution to the archive. This turns out to be the bulk of it, which spans the years 1900 to 1965.

On my second visit to the archive, I chatted with Kathy Marquis, then the university's reference archivist:

Do you know anything about Albert Ingalls?
He had been getting these things in the mail for quite a while and they formed a mass in his files. He decided to get rid of them but didn't want to throw them out. So he donated them to M.I.T.

Is this material still being collected?
No, but when people's personal papers are donated to the archives, time and time again we'll find they kept a "crank file." It will be filed in the C's right next to "Committee on . . ." or whatever. We also receive unsolicited submissions from people who, amazingly enough, want their work to be part of an Archives of Useless Research. Some just say, "What do you think?" They're dying for contact. If you wanted to ask them about their theories, they'd love it.

Has your contact with the material changed your own perceptions of fringe beliefs?
What's fascinating is seeing the themes over and over again, and I've pretty much clarified three of them. One is discomfort with religion and science, and that can go either way. They can either make up their own religious theories or they make up their own scientific theories. But the scientific theories have religious overtones, and the religious theories take in science somehow, sort of like Creationism. And another theme is debunking, you know, Einstein was all wrong, Newton was all wrong, Copernicus was all wrong—and *I'm right.* And the third group is people who want to solve the world riddle in two pages and don't care whether it's provable. It's true because they say it's true.

Do you have any favorites?
The one that always comes to mind is the "Do We Live On the Inside of the Earth?" It catches your fancy because it's so preposterous. It's also something I can comprehend. I'm not a geologist or an astrophysicist, but I have a good idea that we're not living inside the Earth. Whereas some people throw out formulas that I have no way of evaluating.

Why do people formulate these theories?
What's interesting about this collection is that clearly people are fascinated by the craziness of it. But it's not off the spectrum—it's *on* the spectrum. It shows how we feel about forces that are bigger than us, or that we feel powerless against. These people have taken the power back to themselves by redefining science, rather than letting themselves be defined by it. I'd call it crazy if you have to put a label on it, but it's their way of making sense of the world.

leadership

 How to Become a Cult Guru

It wasn't until she met the "sweetly enthusiastic" Lisa Carver of Rollerderby *that Jaina Davis mustered the energy to create her own zine, filling it with peeves, lingerie, clowns, and office supply lust. "The next thing I knew I was walking into stores clutching the first issue of* **FLATTER!***, meekly asking if they'd carry it," she recalls. Each issue of Jaina's journal of oblate puffery has a theme such as "Cakes and Spankings," "Japanese-Jewish," or "Money and Mail." For the cult issue, she asked her first subscriber, Phil X. Milstein, how to start her own.*

Becoming a cult leader is not as tough as you might think. All it takes is a little bit of charisma and some insecure, feeble-minded followers. The reasons you might want to become one are many: it pays well (and all of it tax-exempt), you get lotsa nookie, you can get other people to do your laundry, etc. As a cult guru it's difficult to get health insurance, but that's about the only downside to a career as a leader of men, women, and bastard offspring. What follows, then, is a set of E-Z instructions by which you can soon amass your own group of pasty-faced, glassy-eyed, sycophantic no-hopers who will do your bidding for you.

Rule #1: Confidence = Charisma

To be a messiah you don't have to be tall (Charles Manson was only 5'2"), you don't have to be smart (David Koresh had an I.Q. of 89), and you don't have to be good-looking (though it doesn't hurt). All you have to be is confident, to the absolute. Once you've established your basic set of core beliefs—your schtick, as it were—entertain no doubts and brook no arguments. No matter how ridiculous your premises may be, they are truth, and, by extension, so are you. Remember that deep inside, everyone you meet is like a scrawny branch wavering in the stiff wind of life, just waiting for a big tree to sprout up alongside and protect them. Be that tree.

ZINE VOICES

"When we launched *bOING bOING*, I was a mechanical engineer and designed one of about 100 parts. I was the motor guy. The engineer next to me was the flex lead guy. On Fridays we'd go to lunch with the actuator guy and the spacer ring guy and talk about sports and imported cars. I needed some kind of creative outlet, so Carla and I decided to start *bOING bOING*. I love zines because one person can be responsible for all 100 parts."

—Mark Frauenfelder

Rule #2: Charisma is Relative

To be charismatic, you don't have to be JFK or Madonna. There will always be people more impressionable than you, and as long as you can find those people you too can have charisma, even if those feebs are the only ones who sense it. This has been the key to the cult equation from Christ to Koresh.

Rule #3: Develop Your Schtick

It is no longer sufficient for the potential guru to simply spout chapter and verse from the King James. People can get that stuff anywhere—there's way too much competition in the straight Jesus field, and most of the others are much better at it than you'll ever be. The trick is to find an angle, some niche, and it needn't even involve the Good Book.

Keep in mind that it doesn't really matter what tripe you feed your troupe, so long as you feed it to them with unswerving conviction. I read about one guru down in Australia who has nine wives and sixty-nine children, and all he ever sermonizes about are equal rights for women and Hawaiian culture! According to a *Vanity Fair* article about cults, the nineteenth-century colony leader Rev. Thomas Lake Harris preached to his flock that "a race of tiny fairies inhabited women's breasts, with kings and queens in the left breast and priests and priestesses in the right." And people fell for it.

Armageddon is always an excellent linchpin around which to hang a schtick. One cult out in California is building several rocketships, the better with which to escape the coming End Times. Elizabeth Clare Prophet's Church Universal and Triumphant, like most of the major kook outfits, is also predicting that the end of the world is imminent. She has hundreds if not thousands of followers nestled into the mountains of Montana, with an underground fortress that could sustain them for months. They are armed to the eyeballs and are poised to blow sky-high as soon as Prophet says the word.

But Prophet's teachings are nothing more than a pu-pu platter of world religion, grabbing a little bit from Jesus, a little from Mohammed, a little from Buddha. Her many marks buy it, and they eat it up. There's an audience of willing believers out there for almost any kind of manifesto. Take one that already exists, add a few elements from another, twist it into your own words and—*presto!*, you've got a dogma worthy of any small band of mayonnaise-eaters. Try telling people you're the reincarnation of Mahatma Gandhi and you've been brought back to earth to preach the *Encyclopedia Brittanica.* Or that Albert Einstein comes to you every night to interpret the Quran. Use your imagination and, above all, believe in what you say with everything you've got.

Rule #4: Finding the Feebs

Locating your marks is one of the easiest steps in building a cult, because they practically grow on trees. A favored method is to figure out a particular personality type that might be most prone to fall for your schtick, and pursue that type exclusively.

To paraphrase Elvis, white trash is as white trash does, there's no in-between, you're either with

it all the way or you've blown the scene. In other words, try the Laundromat. Down at the local suds parlor you'll find oodles of brain-dead scum, just sitting around twiddling their thumbs and spittin' pumpkin seeds. Perfect cult fodder. An idle comment can lead to an innocuous conversation, which can lead to a subtle introduction to your confidence, your magnetism, and, ultimately, your compound. Play your cards carefully and you can put out three or four successful invitations to your next communal dinner and/or prayer session per load of laundry. And before long they'll be doing your laundry for you.

You needn't end your search at the Laundromat, of course. Go where the feebs go, especially places where they're likely to have enough time on their hands to hear you out. Bingo parlors are good. Little League games, too. Bowling alleys and pool halls. White-bread church services. BBQ pits. Seek out those who seem to be alone, and those who act like whipped pups. Manson preyed on teenage hitchhikers (though you won't find too many of them these days); Koresh went after Australians. Again, use your imagination; think like your potential victims think. Don't rule out ethnics. And above all, remember that no matter how dumb you are, most of the population is even stupider, so almost everyone you meet is worth your consideration.

Rule #5: Winning Them Over

Having selected your prey, you can now begin to pinpoint a formula approach for that type. Brainwashing is okay, I suppose, but it merely attacks the person's superficial belief system, so it's inadequate for long-term devotion. To truly capture the body you must first capture the mind, and step one is to figure out your mark's weaknesses. Think big—decide if they're insecure, alienated, feeling unloved, etc. A big fat juicy sucker will most likely exhibit symptoms of all of these and more, and be ripe for the picking. The specific weaknesses will differ from person to person, so stay flexible, but you should be able to select one general scheme and apply it to everyone.

Whatever your potential followers' needs are, give to them in grand, exaggerated gestures. If they want for food and shelter, provide them with sumptuous meals and a comfortable bed, and make sure they know they can stay as long as they like. If it's love they long for, you cannot possibly show them too much of it, and passing a little pussy their way couldn't hurt, either. If it's spiritual fulfillment they're after, go all-out with the holy-holy routine, and don't rule out speaking in tongues—it's hard to come up with a convincing counter to somebody speaking in tongues. If lack of self-esteem is the problem, tell them over and over again how good they are, how worthy of being alive. Lie as much as seems necessary, and don't be afraid to pounce on any and every vulnerability they might display.

Those already won over to your way will be most helpful in seducing new recruits. Making your group seem like the happy family the poor schmuck undoubtedly never had will quickly fool him or her into believing wholly in everything you say. During the indoctrination phase, gradually begin giving them chores to do, thus making some use of them while also keeping them too busy to question what's happening to them.

Before long you will have the poor sap primed to do anything you say, even to die for you. Unless you rescued them from the gutter, they should have some money and worldly possessions that can be signed over to you. If they are pleasing to the eye and approximately of the gender of your preference, then so much the better—you've got another sex slave for your harem.

Rule #6: Sticking Around

Being a sane, grounded individual, you do not want to go up in a blaze of apocalyptic glory—not yet, anyway. You have found the perfect occupation to suit your meager skills, and you intend to keep the ball in play for as long as possible. Achieving this takes gaining a certain measure of legitimacy, as antagonizing the authorities could cause more trouble than necessary.

In the cult game, the simple equation is: Longevity + Growth = Legitimacy. Simply sticking around, all the while gradually adding numbers to your membership rolls, is just about all it takes to keep the heat off your back. The Roman Catholic Church is nothing more than a cult that's managed to stick it out a couple thousand years, and as you slide down the cult chronology the legitimacy level slides down accordingly. At the next level are the acceptable Protestant churches: your Lutherans, Methodists, Baptists, Presbyterians, etc. Next level down are those groups that were begun during your grandparents' and great-grandparents' time, such as your Seventh Day Adventists, Mormons, Jehovah's Witnesses, Christian Scientists. These groups by now have earned a certain grudging respect, whereby society in effect says to them, "We don't really like what you do, but you've gotten away with it thus far so we'll let you keep getting away with it."

Down one more step on this evolutionary chain of worship are those cults formed during your and your parents' day: your Scientologists, Moonies, Hare Krishnas, Larouchites. They are ill-regarded by mainstream society, but sects in this category have grown large enough that they are now difficult to fight. In recent years Rev. Moon and Lyndon Larouche have each been convicted of felonies and done hard time in the pokey, while the elusive founder of Scientology, L. Ron Hubbard, was persecuted in absentia for years after he had died! Yet their followings continue to thrive.

Finally, we come to the upstarts. These are the groups that are still officially classified as "cults," and the ones we have mostly dealt with in this guide. They are young, small, hungry, and often nasty. Society hates them. You will be in this category for quite some time, so you'd best keep a low profile for the foreseeable future. If you've got what it takes, you can eventually begin the incremental climb up the ladder of religious respectability. If you do your job real well, perhaps one day your group will find itself joining the world's major religions upon the lofty perch of untouchability. But it won't happen in your lifetime, so don't make it your primary goal.

And that's all there is to it. Six easy steps and you're on your way to a life of leisure and possible immortality. Best of luck, my friend, and may God be with you.

ZINE VOICES

"Why do a zine? Someone dared us to in a drinking game, and we couldn't get dates, so what the hell?"
—Greg Beets and Buzz Moran, *Hey! Hey! Buffet!*

Lists

Twenty–Five Alternative
Ways to Distribute Your Zine

*Every summer during college, I'd return to my base-
ment bedroom and stare at the term papers, clippings, and looseleaf jottings piled in my closet. With
the words of Henry David Thoreau echoing in my
brain ("Simplicity, simplicity, simplicity!"), I dove
in to collate. I set aside the campiest stuff I could find,
pasted it on paper, copied the paper, folded it in half,
affixed stamps, and sent it off to friends. After I graduated, I used* **CHIP'S CLOSET CLEANER** *as an
excuse to write articles I wasn't sure anyone would
want, and to print articles for which that premise
had been confirmed. This list was written after I
became disillusioned with distributors.*

1. Tattoo it to your ass
2. Have stoplight squeegee guys offer a free issue with any purchase
3. Have your representative in Washington read it into the *Congressional Record*
4. Spam it on the Internet using the subject line "How to Find XXX FTP Sites!" or "Make Money Fast!"
5. Read it aloud into your friends' answering machines
6. Print it on dollar bills and go shopping at the Mall of America
7. Print it on business cards and go to a convention
8. Compose it in your head and use ESP
9. Have the CIA drop it on Central American peasants
10. Hand it to tourists in New York City and say it has a map
11. Start a zine mail-order club and offer eight for the price of one
12. Do a Braille edition
13. Only send it to people you've slept with
14. Send people money and tell them if they send it back, they can have a copy of your zine
15. Print it on the back of your high school's diplomas before graduation
16. Write a Top 40 song and use its contents as lyrics
17. Commit a capital crime and as your final statement before your execution, hand your zine out to the media
18. Write your phone number on it and give it to people at bars
19. Trade it with the Amish
20. Print it on Post-It notes and leave reminders for everyone
21. Print it on a T-shirt and wear it until your next issue comes out

22. Convert an old candy machine into a zine dispenser
23. Ask the local porn shop if they'll use it instead of cardboard over the covers of the magazines
24. Leave it under little kids' pillows when they lose a tooth
25. Name your zine "Emergency Instructions" and slip it into airplane seat magazine pockets

Five Weird News Items So Common They're Not Weird Anymore

While working in Washington, D.C., during the Carter years, Chuck Shepherd was caught in the general malaise. He battled back by clipping ironic or funny or strange news articles and pouring them into a zine. Eventually **VIEW FROM THE LEDGE** *spawned Chuck's syndicated column, "News of the Weird." But unlike what newspaper editors get from him,* VFTL *includes Chuck's caustic commentary. He recently compiled this list of weird news items that he sees so often they bore him.*

1. Images of Jesus or Mary spotted on the rusty door of an old appliance, a billboard ad for pizza, the markings on the hide of a cow, or the side of a town's water tower.

2. Bank robbers who write hold-up notes on the back of one of their personalized checks or deposit slips, or on the postcard advising them of their next scheduled appointment with their parole officer, or on a loan application they filled out while working up the nerve to pull off the heist.

3. Motor-trip errors by Mom, Dad, and the kids who discover about 100 miles down the road that an inadequate head count after the last rest stop has resulted in one or more missing family members.

4. Continuing pet acquisitions in small homes until such time as the neighbors begin to worry about the smell and the authorities are called in wearing gas masks in order to remove the emaciated animals and to clean the floor of feces—and after, neighbors describe the home's owner as a "nice person" but a "loner."

5. Men found in shock with part or all of their genitals missing, swearing that some man-hating prostitute cut them, or that there was a serious industrial accident, or that a zipper performed improperly. Later, it is discovered that, almost always, the injury was the result of a serious masturbatory error involving household equipment of some kind.

Final Exits for Aquatic Species

*"As long as I remember," says Don Steinberg, "I've been thrilled by the idea that you could write something down, hand it to someone, and they would laugh." He and his brother Steve published their first zine—*Slopp—*in elementary school; they founded* **MEANWHILE . . .** *in 1991 as a showcase for their writing and wit.*

(arranged in approximate order of funniness)

OCTOPUS—*slit wrists*

FLYING FISH—*jump onto bridge*

SWORDFISH—*hara-kiri*

BLUEFISH—*tranquilizer overdose*

ELECTRIC EEL—*pull the plug*

TWELVE-POUND BASS—*public hanging*

STINGRAY—*carbon monoxide*

PUFFER—*self-asphyxiation*

BLOWFISH—*cocaine OD*

RAINBOW TROUT—*bad acid*

BONEFISH—*calcium deficiency*

SHARK—*hunger strike*

HERMIT CRAB—*exposure*

ANGEL FISH—*martyrdom*

PERCH—*knock self off*

SEAHORSE—*break leg*

HAMMERHEAD SHARK—*blunt instrument*

TRIGGER FISH—*shoot self after sniping spree*

SOCKEYE SALMON—*concussion*

KISSING GOURAMI—*herpes*

SNAPPER—*lose all control*

SUN FISH—*immolation*

LOBSTER—*cholesterol*

STARFISH—*career suicide*

Jim and Mr. Peanut

As part of a literary section in the third issue of **MEANWHILE . . .**, *Steve Steinberg introduced an unexpected character to a familiar tale. Mark Twain would be proud.*

I reckon it was long past noon when I finally woke. The sun was fixing to head back down past the trees and the bugs was starting to take a real shining to my face. I decided it warn't no good to jes set there on the raft and be eaten live, so's I figured I'd go wake our newest travelin' companion and see if he knew something bout some food. He was a queer looking sort, and I got mighty nervous and fidgety before shaking him. Y'see, I done my share of getting around, but I jes never seen nothing like this one. He didn't have what me and you might call a head and then a neck and then a chest and then a belly, like most folks. What he done had was jes a big peanut for a body; a big old peanut-man body and skinny little arms and legs.

Truth be, I's the one din't want him on the raft when he swam by round midnight. Jim's the one to start talkin bout all of us being God's creatures and other Sunday school rot and pretty soon my conscience got me to agree. We's both powerful scared, though, when he began a'talkin.

"My name is Mister Peanut." He warn't from these parts I could tell by his talking. He sounded like acting folk, only I knew he couldn't be no actor looking like that. I spose I woulda laughed if I wasn't so afeared. Jim jes set there like he was lookin at the devil's ghost inna flesh.

"You see, my fine lads," Peanut said rightin his one eye-glass and tall hat, "the South is just no place for a sophisticated legume."

Jim was whiter than the bottom of a plucked hen, jes mumblin "fisticated lay-goon" over and over at hisself.

Even though I was dog tired, sleep dint come too powerful easy. I reckon I was busy decidin in my mind ifs or not I should roll our sleepin peanut goblin off the raft. Also, I's busy figurin what I'd look like in that fancy society-folk hat a his.

Between the Lines

A stand-up comedian and satirist, Paul Krassner has been called "the father of the underground press" by People *magazine. Is that an honor? He founded* **THE REALIST** *in 1958 and plans to continue until the year 2000. This selection is taken from the "Court Jester" column that opens each issue.*

When I was a kid, I imprinted on certain phrases I would hear my parents utter. These phrases might well have been clichés—excuse me, shopworn clichés—but they were fresh to me. When my father talked about the law of supply and demand, it became a filter for my understanding of all human behavior. When my mother said, "nothing ventured, nothing gained," I took it as a daily omen.

I didn't read my first complete book until I was twenty-one. I got all through high school and college by reading the material in italics the night before an exam. I based book reports on *Classic Comics*. In my report on *Hamlet*, I described how at the end he stabs himself and says, "Aarrggh!!"

I kept buying books the whole time and never reading them. But I would practice a kind of mystical bibliomancy. I would put my index finger into the pages and zero in on a particular passage. So, for example, although I never read Aldous Huxley's novel, *Antic Hay*, I can tell you that on page 115 of the paperback edition, there is a phrase—"excruciating orgasms of self-assertion"—which began to serve as yet another filter to understand all human behavior.

I now own thousands of books I haven't read, and I continue to buy new ones. It must be some kind of strange psychological disease. The latest book I bought is a biography of Aldous Huxley by Sybille Bedford, 741 pages that I'll probably never read. But I did zero in on a passage where, in 1956, Huxley described the animal experiments at UCLA:

> . . . rats and cats and monkeys with electrodes stuck into various areas of their brains. They press a little lever which gives them a short, mild electric shock—and the experiment is evidently so ecstatically wonderful, that they will go on at a rate of 8,000 self-stimuli per hour until they collapse from exhaustion, lack of food and sleep. We are obviously getting very close to reproducing the Moslem paradise where every orgasm lasts 600 years.

I didn't know *that*. No wonder they have such a big army in Iraq. They're really motivated. In our culture, heaven would be having television that always gets good reception.

Oh, well. If there is a heaven, my father is there. Before he died, I told him how his talking about the law of supply and demand had influenced me so strongly.

"Aw," he said, "I don't believe in that anymore. . . ."

Lounge

The Color of Lounge

Each week, Benjamin Serrato's **15 MINUTES** *blankets Austin with quarter-hour reads such as the horrible ways famous writers have met their deaths, the history of Legos, and a beginner's guide to the alleys ("I enjoy bowling with people who aren't offended that I select a ball by its color"). In this selection, Marcy Shapiro goes paint shopping.*

Having decided that the junk room in my house would be more serviceable to me as a lounge, I began a quest for the perfect red paint to cloak my walls. After spending twenty-five minutes alone at Builder's Hell and not discovering a shade remotely worthy of lounge, I sought out the Mr. Builder's Hell Paint Guy.

"Do you mix paints?"

"Yep."

"So can I describe the color I want and you'll mix it?"

"You want to describe the color?"

"Yeah."

I had imagined the red I craved. It conjured up the smell of sex, the feel of velvet, the yearning for another Scotch, the desire to slip off your shoes, and maybe some items of clothing. It was the red of The Lounge, of danger and heat and comfort. It was the kind of red that makes you look beautiful and not care that the person next to you doesn't.

"So if I describe it . . ."

"You can't describe it. You have to bring in a swatch."

"I don't have a swatch."

"Then bring in a paint chip."

"But I've never seen this red. I just know it exists somewhere."

"Come back with a paint chip."

"You won't even listen to my description?"

"This is a hardware store, not some psychic paint convention."

Determined, I headed to Sears. Not only did it not have the perfect red, it didn't have anything near red. For the record, Sears only sells preapproved, preordained beige and fourteen shades of white.

The next stop was Breeder's Square. When I asked for the most carnal red they had, the Paint Master handed me a swatch of Cardinal Red.

"Cardinal like the pope?" I asked. It looked rather harmless.

"Actually, a member of the Sacred Church, which elects the Pope."

"I'm Jewish. I can't have anything to do with the Pope. What I want is carnal sin."

"I don't think it has anything to do with religion. Let me ask my manager. Hey, Frank, what color is Cardinal Red?"

"Carnal Red?"

"No, Cardinal Red."

"Deep scarlet."

"See, it has nothing to do with religion."

"Well, can I have Cardinal only more so?"

"Only more what?"

"More carnal."

"Ma'am, this is a family store."

Lowering my voice and making sure the manager had split, I approached the Paint Master on another level.

"I'll give you twenty bucks to sex up this paint."

Taking the money from my palm, the man had obviously made his decision.

"Give me two gallons," I said.

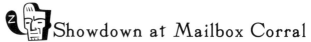

Showdown at Mailbox Corral

BUBBA'S LIVE BAIT, *assembled in Knoxville, U.S.A., by Alphonse Coleman and Qathy Googloo, is a scrapbook of political rants, grumpy vs. groovy lists, telemarketing confessions, found text, and tantalizing tales of mystery and mayhem. So sit back and settle in, cause it's time for Alphonse to spin a yarn.*

Some people may not have heard of it, but if it was an Olympic sport, Tennessee would get the gold. Of what do I speak? Mailbox baseball, of course! Before I tell my little anecdote, let me fill you in. When you are in high school in Blountville, Tennessee, there is very little to do. So you get a fake ID and buy beer and—you guessed it—drink and drive!

Now don't start preaching at me, ya pansies—we knew it was stupid, that's half the reason we did it. The other half was baseball. We'd get wasted, get a coupla bats and smash people's mailboxes to hell. Sometimes people we knew (friends, ex-bosses, principals), sometimes strangers. The driver of the car would slow down to 35 mph or so, the passenger would lean out the window, the driver would swerve real close to the postal victim, and then—BAM! Home run! Sometimes for extra special jobs (or if the driver wanted to get in on the action), you'd stop and everyone would get out and wail on the box L.A.P.D. style.

Like any sport, you had to have special equipment. In mailbox baseball, it was your bat. As a player, you had to be at one with your bat. You had to know its every whim. Usually an aluminum bat was a no-no, unless you wanted to be vibrating with the shock for weeks. Some guys had regular wooden bats, some would saw it off a bit, one guy used a sawed-off pool cue (he was bit of a philistine). I had a wooden T-ball bat. It was the perfect length (with a long bat you risk taking out the car windows). It was taped on the shaft with black electrician's tape and on the handle with a grip to absorb some of the shock and make it easier to hold (we're talking some stiff impacts). Burnt into the wood just above the grip was its name: SPECIAL DELIVERY. Oh, how I miss that bat!

Anyway, my brother apparently got into a "you bash mine, I'll bash yours" standoff over mailboxes. (Now pay attention, because this will help illustrate the futility of the arms race, among other lessons.) They dent his, he dents theirs, they beat the crap outta his, he does likewise. Soon these fellas run over our mailbox with a truck, so he uproots theirs and runs over it too. They uproot ours back and beat it up and set it on fire.

After going through all of these mailboxes (they ain't cheap, either), my brother finally adopted a new tactic. He went to the store and got one of those three-foot-tall, two-foot-wide monster mailboxes. He then put a smaller, regular-size mailbox inside it (for the mail) and poured in some cement. He also dug a five-foot hole with some post-diggers, stuck a railroad tie in it and poured more concrete to fill the base. With some help (it weighed like 200 pounds), he mounted the box-cemented-inside-a-box on the tie with some giant bolts. When the door was closed it looked just like any other mailbox.

Soon enough, the boys were back with their bats. The first time they drove by quite fast and one of the guys reached out and smacked the box with the bat. He severely sprained his wrist and shattered his bat. The mailbox stood unscathed. They came back in frustration and shot it several times with a shotgun. The boom echoed through the valley. The mailbox was dinked.

A few days later they returned again. This time, they figured, they wouldn't bother with the box but just run it down with the truck. They hit it at 5 or 10 mph, but even at that speed, meeting a brick wall can be traumatic. The truck's bumper and grille crumpled like crepe paper. The mailbox stood like a monolith.

They tried a few other tactics, like filling it full of cherry bombs, and tying a rope around it and trying to yank it over with the truck, but it was all for naught. Eventually, they just plum up and quit. The box is still there. Sure, its paint is flaking, its sides are full of buckshot, the post has some chrome flecks on it, and the inside smells faintly of gunpowder—but it stands as a testimony to the only life strategy that really works: Be as strong as you can and they will eventually stop trying to break you. Can you believe I managed to come to that conclusion from a story about bored rednecks smashing things? Bubba say: "Aggression is no substitute for a solid foundation!"

movies

A History of the Drivers' Education Film

When he was in high school, Ralph Coon wrote movie reviews for the student paper. But rather than analyzing Hollywood's best, he dissected the educational films that teachers showed in class. "The films that got the most word-of-mouth were from drivers' education," he says. "Stories of cheerleaders vomiting and football jocks fainting ripped through the halls like wildfire." In 1991, using notes he had taken years earlier, Ralph began to track down the men who made these stark films. A cranky Earl J. Deems, who made nineteen of the bloodfests, hung up on Ralph twice but finally granted the interview that became the backbone of **THE LAST PROM***, named after Ralph's favorite example of the genre. Subsequent issues, equally as good as the first, have profiled fanatical TV preacher Dr. Gene Scott and influential UFO researcher Gray Barker.*

Ostensibly taught by professionals, drivers' education is often, especially in rural school systems, overseen by gym teachers. Before or during their sophomore year, high school students are yanked off the playing fields and placed in darkened classrooms. They watch with trepidation as a scratched and brittle 16mm film travels noisily through a projector, bringing to the screen a uniquely American learning tradition: the drivers' education film.

The 1950 film, "The Last Date," is typical of the drivers' ed movies that reached classrooms for the first time in the late forties and early fifties. Jeanie, a beautiful teenager, must chose between two boyfriends. Larry always drives courteously and observes the speed limit, while Nick (played by a young Dick York) drives his hot rod insanely fast. At a high school dance, Jeanie ditches Larry and slips out unnoticed with Nick for a moonlit drive. As they speed along, a disc jockey on the radio urges teenagers not to commit "teenicide, the fine art of killing yourself with an automobile before you turn twenty." The words echo in Jeanie's head as Nick barrels around a corner, smashing into an oncoming car.

Educators were quick to realize that the hokiness of these films made them a laughable, high-camp good time—just as they are today—and detracted from the message. Because of this, dri-

---

ZINE VOICES

"When I first saw *Factsheet Five,* I had never heard of zines. The concept charmed me. Was it legal? Could just anyone do it? I sent off for a few. Some were brilliant, some were boring, some were perverted, some were so personal they made me sigh. Inspired, I wrote some things and drew some things and glued some things down. Then I made seven copies—five for the zine people I'd met, one for my family and one for a spare."

—Maria Goodman, *Don't Say Uh-Oh!*

vers' education pictures became rougher toward the end of the fifties. Much rougher.

The 1958 Canadian film, "Safety or Slaughter," was among the first to include authentic scenes of highway fatalities. "I'd like to show you a few statistics," intones the monotonic narrator. "That man is a statistic. So is that girl. These are real people, just like you and me." The carnage is brief, but effective.

In the following year, Dick Wyman, a still photographer from Mansfield, Ohio, lost a friend to an automobile accident and decided to use his abilities to help prevent further loss of life.

After purchasing primitive 16mm film equipment, he began riding in the back of ambulances, filming accident victims. Wyman named his first film after the Ohio State Highway Patrol's official code for a fatal crash, "Signal 30." No one seemed interested. Undaunted, he made several more crash pictures. Still no one showed interest. It appeared as though Wyman's embryonic style of shock therapy drivers' training was terminal before it ever got legs.

In reality, the golden age of drivers' education films was about to begin.

Wyman's accountant, Earl J. Deems, offered to purchase the rights to his films. To lend credibility to the venture, Deems forged a symbiotic relationship with the Ohio State Highway Patrol. Deems also recognized and made use of the lucrative English-speaking overseas market, selling "Signal 30" and other films to military installations.

Deems' work paid off and in the early sixties he formed his own company, Highway Safety Films, Inc. Over the next fourteen years, Deems churned out nineteen of the most hideously authentic crash films ever made. Now seventy-one and retired from filmmaking, Deems still resides in Mansfield. Although it's been nearly twenty years since he completed his last film, he still receives phone calls from educators searching for his movies. "I always felt I was doing a big service," he says in his husky voice. "People grew up watching my films and now some have become teachers and police officers who want to show them to their students."

People did indeed grow up watching Deems' work. Three of his films, "Mechanized Death," "Wheels of Tragedy," and "Highways of Agony," are among the most well-remembered of drivers' education films.

Deems declines to discuss the budgets of his films. He will say, however, that when actors were needed for films like "Wheels of Tragedy" (one of his few that relied on reenactments), he recruited amateurs from nearby dinner theaters. Deems would also sometimes invite wreck victims to lecture viewers.

"Drive to Survive" and "A Matter of Judgement" were among his later films. With them, he continued his idiomatic combination of gore and purple-prose narration. "This young teenager tried to outrun a train. Now he won't ever outrun anything again," pronounces an overbearing narrator while rescue workers pry a mutilated corpse from a car-train collision.

Deems insists that few viewers ever complained about his macabre teaching tactics. "Most people I heard from told me, 'Way to go,' " he says. However, the filmmaker is quick to point out that he knew where to draw the line. "I left some old footage out. There was no reason to show a decapitation. What would the point of that be? In those cases I lingered on the mangled automobile."

In 1979 Deems completed his swan song, "Options to Live," reiterating his place as one of the founders of realism-based drivers' education. "We're Highway Safety Films, Inc.," a narrator seated in an editing room informs us. "Since 1959 we've taken you to the scenes of countless highway traffic accidents. We've included some of the most shocking scenes ever put on motion picture film. We have shown you the injured, the dying, and the dead. Do you remember us?" The film cuts to images of a truck driver impaled against his steering wheel, expired drivers curled up on the asphalt after being catapulted hundreds of feet from their vehicles, accident scenes where it is impossible to distinguish car from driver. "Now I'll bet you remember us," the narrator concludes triumphantly.

Without a doubt, "Options to Live" is the cataclysmic apex of the genre. In it, Deems utilizes a new technique, one that could shock even the most hardened of viewers: the sounds of an accident scene. Moans of the dying drowned out by the shriek of sirens dot the film's soundtrack. "My legs, my legs," one woman screams after noticing her neatly severed leg lying next to her.

With the marriage of sound and visuals, Deems may well have taken his brand of shock therapy over the top. Soon after the release of "Options to Live," Highway Safety Film's activities mysteriously ceased. Rumors circulated that the company was forced out of business due to legal complications from accident victims caught on film who demanded a cut of Deems' profits.

The truth was that in 1980 and 1981 Deems shot footage for one more film, tentatively titled, "Strategies for Safe Driving." But while editing the film in 1983, his wife lost a battle with cancer. Deems shelved "Strategies for Safe Driving" and retired.

Sadly, Deems may be the sole curator of his work. Most schools and police departments have removed the films from their catalogs. Even the National Safety Council, a non-profit organization designed to promote and distribute instructional safety films, has categorized Deems' films as "dead storage," more than likely never to see the light of a projector bulb again. Videophiles have long been circulating copies of Deems' more notorious films. But most are poorly dubbed, eighth- or ninth-generation copies and barely watchable.

Once Deems retired, the Ohio State Highway Patrol was without its singular supplier of films. So it created a media division to produce its own. Among its first works was "End Result," a collage of fatal accidents set to music. However, the demand was so strong for Deems' films that a series of remakes was scheduled. According to a source within the department, "Signal 30 II" was shot in the late eighties. But during its editing a new regime took over and dismissed the project, opting instead to make a Batman parody called "Buckleman." Buckleman drives around in his Bucklemobile and zaps people not wearing safety belts with his bucklegun, immediately strapping them in.

Unlike the Ohio Highway Patrol, few police departments have the money to produce their own films. Most rely on slide presentations of local traffic accidents. There are exceptions. The California Highway Patrol has been producing films since the late sixties. Their first production, "Red Asphalt," is perhaps the most infamous of all drivers' education films.

Started in 1965 and finished four years later, "Red Asphalt" was photographed by a camera club from Hollywood, according to the film's producer, Kemp Milton, who now works for the National Highway Safety Administration. "That's why it took four years to shoot. Most of the time the volunteers would get there late and the victims would be gone. How many films can you make about two wrecked cars?"

"Red Asphalt" centers around the consequences of an automobile accident when you *aren't* killed. Maimed and mutilated accident victims are carted into ambulances, their lives forever changed. The film proved such a success that two sequels were made, and the California Highway Patrol plans to make another every ten years.

Because most of the blood and guts drivers' education films were nothing more than a compilation of highway accidents, little if any understanding of film techniques were needed to make them. The dramatization film was the arena for displaying cinematic vision, and sadly, few lived up to the challenge. A noteworthy exception was Gene McPherson, director and producer of "The Last Prom."

"The Last Prom" opens on a demolished car resting in front of a small high school. "There is a deadly fascination about a wrecked car," the narrator tells us as the camera cuts to the car's blood-smeared windshield. "Was it a pretty face that made this gaping, jagged hole in the windshield?" The film dissolves into a flashback, telling the story of Bill Donovan, a "good boy, but a bad driver," who attends his high school prom with a friend, Sandy Clark. Following the motif of most "date" drivers' education pictures, Bill and Sandy, along with two friends, leave the dance early to go for a drive. Speeding carelessly along, Bill plows into a tree, hurling Sandy through the windshield, killing her.

Using handheld cameras and washed-out, single-source cinematography, McPherson twists his budgetary inadequacies to his advantage, creating a pseudo-documentary that chillingly makes its point without ever once exploiting a real-life tragedy.

Little is known about the production of "The Last Prom." Judging by the vehicles in the film, it was made around 1972. According to the credits, it was filmed at Anderson High School in Hamilton County, Ohio. The film's creepy a cappella soundtrack is credited to the Anderson High School Vocal Ensemble. It is a stunning, highly effective film, as eerie as any good low-budget horror film, and should be required viewing for any drivers' education aficionados.

With the exception of Earl Deems' pictures, most drivers' education films lie in the public domain. Surely there must be a Kroger Babb protégé lurking out there who can appreciate the commercial possibilities in resurrecting these gems. "Drug menace" films of the thirties like "Reefer Madness" and "Cocaine Fiends" are cult favorites, and documentaries like "Atomic Cafe" and "Heavy Petting" rekindled interest in 1950s propaganda and educational films. Could a film juxtaposing the crimson imagery of "Red Asphalt" with the sheer corniness of "The Last Date" be far off?

Is the world ready?

"After the drivers' education film issue came out, I tracked down the director of 'The Last Prom' and began a correspondence. I told him I intended to remake his film for a new generation. He said such a remake would be expensive, have no audience, and serve absolutely no need. I wrote again, saying I wanted to become the drivers' education filmmaker for the art-house crowd. He never replied."

—Ralph Coon, *The Last Prom*

Drills on Film

The following selection was prepared for In Touch, *a magazine for dental hygienists, but the article fell through because the films all showcase dentists. I submitted it to* **CHIP'S CLOSET CLEANER** *instead, which eerily has never rejected any of my work.*

With National Dental Hygiene Month just around the corner,[1] it seemed like a good time to take a look at some memorable Hollywood dental visits:

Dentist: W.C. Fields
Film: The Dentist (1932)
Patient: Miss Mason
Reason for Visit: Toothache.
Treatment: "Doc" straddles Miss Mason to get pliers grip on bad tooth; dentist and patient bounce scandalously around room.[2]
Outcome? Patient flees.
Best line: "This won't hurt you—much."

Dentist: Biff Grimes (James Cagney)[3]
Film: The Strawberry Blonde (1941)
Patient: William Grimes (Alan Hale Sr.)[4]
Reason for Visit: Biff receives dentistry course in mail and jolly Irish dad offers aching molars as educational tool.
Treatment: Select random tooth to yank after administering nitrous oxide from hobby tank.
Outcome? Unjustly convicted of fraud, Biff finishes coursework in prison.
Best line: "As soon as I get my first patient, I'm going to quit that milk route."

Dentist: Herbie the Elf
Film: Rudolph the Red-Nosed Reindeer (1964)
Patient: Abominable Snowman
Reason for Visit: Sharp incisors threaten protagonists.
Treatment: Yank all after patient pushed over cliff.
Outcome? Herbie opens North Pole practice; Abominable joins forces of good.

Best line: Herbie with Rudolph. "You don't mind my red nose?" "Not if you don't mind me being a dentist." "It's a deal!"

Dentist: Dr. Schatz, a.k.a. Chief Inspector Jacques Clouseau (Peter Sellers)
Film: The Pink Panther Strikes Again (1976)
Patient: Former Chief Inspector Dreyfus (Herbert Lom)
Reason for Visit: Hard candy crushed premolar.
Treatment: Place "special anesthetic cotton wool" over patient's eyes before searching for clues. Share nitrous oxide; place feet on patient's chest for leverage and yank wrong tooth.
Outcome? Clouseau is recognized but escapes despite being doubled over in nitrous oxide-induced laughter.
Best line: "I normally don't mecca hassle calls in the metal of the gnat."

Dentist: Christian Szell (Laurence Olivier)
Film: Marathon Man (1976)
Patient: Gabe Levy (Dustin Hoffman)
Reason for Visit: Nazi Szell tortures Levy while asking cryptically, "Iz it safe?"
Treatment: Dig into cavity, relieve with oil of cloves. Service healthy teeth with aging drill that plugs into wall outlet.
Outcome? Levy triumphs but faces years of dentiphobia.
Best line: "Please don't worry. I'm not going into that cavity . . . a freshly cut nerve is infinitely more sensitive."

Dentist: Dr. Miles (James Noble)
Film: 10 (1979)
Patient: George Webber (Dudley Moore)
Reason for Visit: Smitten with Miles' daughter (Bo Derek), Webber schedules check-up to learn more.
Treatment: Doc finds and fills six cavities.
Outcome? Webber ingests pain pills and brandy for days.
Best line: None, but Bo Derek gets naked later.

Dentist: Sheldon Kornpett (Alan Arkin)
Film: The In-Laws (1979)
Patient: Mrs. Adelman
Reason for Visit: Dentures
Treatment: Patient abandoned as Kornpett runs errand for future in-law, CIA agent Vince Ricardo (Peter Falk).
Outcome? Mouthpiece bonds to patient's teeth.
Best line: Ricardo [as men face Latin American firing squad]: "Spare this man, General. He's a dentist from New York, a city in which there are thousands of Spanish-speaking people who stand in dire need of extensive bridge-work." Kornpett: "That was it?! The dental thing? I'm a dead man!"

[1] February

[2] It is hard to mistake this scene for anything but spirited simulated fucking.

[3] By far the best dentist film of the bunch

[4] Father of Alan Hale Jr., who played the Skipper on "Gilligan's Island"

Rejected Apes Subplots

As part of a tribute to that cinematic classic, The Planet of the Apes, *Rod Lott and Chris Henry of* **HITCH** *ponder what might have been.*

- Dr. Zaius calls for an end to feces-throwing during council meetings.

- The astronauts attempt to teach the apes how to eat a banana without regurgitating it back up.

- A voyage to the Forbidden Zone is temporarily interrupted by the discovery of an old tire hanging by a rope from a tree.

- Dr. Zaius must swallow his pride and ask the humans for help in dealing with a devastating lice epidemic.

- The apes are up in arms when it is learned that their gorilla military leader is actually an oversized gibbon in disguise.

- Violence erupts over who will play the lead in the community theater adaptation of "Welcome to the Monkey House."

- Zira must endure governmental scorn and public apathy in her quest to prove that her human specimens are capable of sign language.

- Cornelius creates a scientific uproar when he postulates that the gorillas actually evolved from professional wrestlers.

- The apes' future is threatened when their land is visited by descendants of Marlon Perkins.

parents

Nice Dad Things

Since its debut in 1994, **DON'T SAY UH-OH!** *has become known as "the zine of lists" (Foods to Eat on a Dare, Why I Get Bad Haircuts, Strange But True Toys, Game Shows I'm Not Making Up). "Sometimes people misinterpret my list-making and send me their ten favorite songs with no reasons for the selections," says editor Maria Goodman. "How could anyone care about that? Whenever a list is personalized with details, someone's bound to identify with it."*

1. One day when I was on my way to work at the pharmacy, which he knew I hated, my dad handed me his pair of yellow night-driving sunglasses and said, "Here, wear these, it'll look sunny out." He knew it sounded dopey but he said it anyway. And even though I felt like a fool I wore them all the cloudy way over to the pharmacy and it did look kind of sunny out.

2. Another depressing day—week—I'd been in my room for hours. I heard my dad get his bike out, clank away, and then come back a few minutes later. He knocked on my door and came in and said, "Look, I got some Crunchies." (Cheetos—more on his made-up brand names later.) He was trying to cheer me up. "Look, I got some of these pop things too," he said, holding up bottles of orange, grape, and red Faygo which he couldn't have known I hated. I took one and smiled and said, "Thanks Dad." He said, "It was hard to balance all that crap on my bike."

3. Sometimes he buys my favorite cereal for no reason. Sometimes he tries to buy my brother's favorite cereal only he gets it wrong and buys the no-brand kind: "Honey Toasted O's" in the cellophane bag instead of "Honey Nut Cheerios" in the box. He hates sugar cereal. "Here, I got you your Sugar-Coated Sugar Cubes," he says.

4. If anybody doesn't feel good, he gets them a blanket. It's the best cure.

5. It makes him very happy if you make cookies. Any kind—"Hey cookies!" he says. When they're cooling he keeps sneaking up to steal some. "I'll test them for ya," he says when caught.

6. Super K Mart is his favorite store and he finds any excuse to go there. He calls from work and asks if we need anything and even if you say, "No, I don't think so," he'll pause and then say, "Well I better pick up some Kleenex" or "Oh, I know, we're low on salt," and he'll stop on his way home. Sometimes early in the morning he goes there because it's open 24 hours. "I went to Super K Mart at 7 A.M. and got bananas," he says. If you ever accompany him you will not come out for at least three hours, because he likes to go up and down every row "just to look."

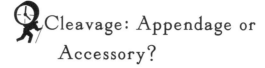

Cleavage: Appendage or Accessory?

For those of you who have never been pawed, pawholes are what happens when you're wearing jeans that have little rips in the butt and someone "paws and paws you all night and by the end of the night you have huge gaping pawholes where those chaste little rips were." Needless to say, **PAWHOLES** *is better as a zine than a fashion statement. Launched in 1991, recent issues of Deborah Barkun and Keren Kurti's feminist reader have included an interview with the owner of a sex toy shop, calls for the popularization of words like poontang and booboisie, and creative revenge techniques to use against ex-boyfriends (one involves pubic hair, tape, and an index card). This selection, with an introduction by Deborah, first appeared in issue 5.*

This past winter I found myself departing western Pennsylvania to traverse the flatlands of the Midwest for a promising rendezvous with a man. On the eve of my trip, a co-worker inquired as to what I was going to wear. Always the punk chick, I pointed out my well-worn Levi's, a black T-shirt, and my lucky purple suede belt. "Ahhh," she cooed, gesturing toward my rather ample and bounteous 32DD bosom. "You'll be well-suited, *and* well-accessorized."

I must admit I've never considered my breasts to be a fashion accessory. When I run, they're a hindrance, arriving at the 10K mark before the rest of me despite their entrapment in that steel-plated, Viking-style jog-bra. Long ago I learned that it was futile to stuff my overflowing flesh into any lacy bit of finery that Victoria secreted away. My last boyfriend announced early on in our dubious coupledom that he never considered himself a "breast man" and "no offense, but I prefer the waif look." Needless to say, I've since rid myself of *that* cumbersome appendage.

I heeded the advice of my colleague that evening and clad myself in my finest pair of breasts. As the temperate northern air kissed my abundant cleavage, I was enlightened to the world of haute couture. Women from all walks of life are versed in the appendage vs. accessory conundrum, which nursed the following collection of titillating tales of both the boob-friendly and nipples-as-nemesis variety. Unhook, relax, and enjoy:

Sue, rocker

I used to play guitar in the middle-school jazz band. It met at 7 A.M. I would always be sleepy and sit hunched over my guitar. Two boys nearby would snicker and ask if I had the guitar custom made. I didn't get it for the longest time. Then I realized that my right breast rested in the curve of the guitar. So I began to reply, "Yes, this guitar is a 34B."

When I was a photo student, I was consumed with photographing myself. In the course of one endeavor in my bedroom, I was using a Sun Gun (a bright, hot electric lamp) on a rickety tripod. Since the photographs were to be submitted to someone who would judge them as "art" and give me a grade, I was nude.

Somehow I managed to kick over the Sun Gun. During my annual gynecological exam, which took place the following week, I explained why I had a blistered left nipple. The nurse said that "It" looked as if "It" was healing nicely. Then she handed me a stack of literature about abusive relationships. She also said that I shouldn't feel badly about "It" and that stories to cover "It" up weren't necessary.

I changed nurses three times after that, and each one gave me the same pamphlets. I finally found one who believed me. She gave me no literature. I have a lovely iridescent scar on my left nipple.

Dee-Dee, cuisine service engineer

I am a waitress. My apron lands just above my nipples. If tied securely, it acts like a corset. The upper half of my breasts swell above the top while the rest of their mass rounds behind the fabric, adding a plump ripeness to the screen-printed fruits. I tie my apron loosely, and it shifts constantly as I sashay about the restaurant. While one breast is always covered, the other boldly reaches out, like an extra appendage. Unable to look away, my customers stare with horror, wonder, excitement, and hunger. With a quick hook of my thumb I realign my apron and continue to greet, engage, smile, offer, present, bend, lean, lift, kneel, and feed.

One evening as I went about my serving ways, playing a constant game of peek-a-boob, my body asserted itself. I brought the food on a cocktail tray that I held close to my body. When I reached the last item, a bowl of soup, I was confronted with my right breast. Like a garnish, it sat atop the creamy broth. Although it was attached to my body, it seemed to float alone. I thought that perhaps it would remain in the bowl when I lifted it to the table, and a hungry mouth might nurse soup from it. For a long moment I was unable to move, afraid of losing my breast.

The spell was finally broken when the eldest woman at the table spoke. "Oh dear, it looks like you got a little on yourself."

Deborah, frustrated proletarian

My freshman two-dimensional design course was taught by an aging pedagogue named Walter. Walter had assigned each student a color combination and asked each of us to bring a still life to class. I received red and green, so I set up two tomatoes on a cloth. I arranged my pallet and began the task of depicting the vegetables. As we worked, Walter circulated, criticizing each lackluster study. I continued to paint in silence until he reached my pallet. "What luscious, ripe tomatoes you have, Deborah!" he boomed. My face ripened from green to red.

Last Saturday I was doing my weekly shopping in the Strip District, Pittsburgh's famed produce yards. I passed by a cut flower stand with a sign, "U-Pick-'em, We'll Wrap-'em." A crusty old flower merchant called out to me: "Hey baby! U-Stack-'em, I'll Pack-'em!" Brilliant!

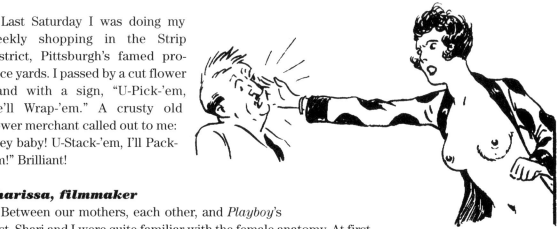

Charissa, filmmaker

Between our mothers, each other, and *Playboy*'s best, Shari and I were quite familiar with the female anatomy. At first glance, the *Cosmo* she pulled out that day wasn't particularly interesting. Then I saw what she was hysterical over. "How To Get Rid of Unwanted Nipple Hair." I thought, "How could they? How could something as beautiful as breasts grow unsightly and unwanted hair?"

Each hair is to be plucked out with tweezers just as if it were an eyebrow, followed by an immediate rubdown to close the pore. The article said nothing about why a breast might sprout hair.

We thought that it must be a trick. Between the two of us we had seen a lot of boobs, yet never once did we spot nipple hair. As far as we could remember, no one had ever even spoken the words nipple and hair in the same sentence. That's when Shari told me her father said eating onions made hair grow on your chest.

I often wonder if *Cosmo* didn't have a strange effect on my opinion of the body. However, if a survey is being taken, I love my breasts. They are such a great part of the body. I don't remember the day I first got nipple hair, or that gentle pinch and oooh soothing rub, but I do remember that frantic afternoon.

Moe, skipper

I was born second in a family of four daughters. After Molly grew from an A to a C cup before her freshman year, we watched her come to breakfast holding one arm beneath her breasts to prevent their painful jostling.

There was a family phrase for mammary development: "to go Baboomba!" My mother went Baboomba! the year she turned fifteen, while she and her family were in Germany visiting the village where her parents were born. For months afterward, a vicious rumor circulated that Louise had gotten an operation, and all the girls crowded her in the locker room trying to see the scars.

My three sisters all went Baboomba! turn by turn, but I never did. My breasts are a little bigger than a handful, the left a little larger than the right. My nipples spread out flat like big pink coins and they are wonderfully sensitive. I had the right one pierced.

Working on fishing boats and being the only one with breasts can be lonely, but I like to shake up my nineteen-year-old crew mates by waking up and saying: "Man, my tits are sore." They never have anything to add.

TALKING DICK

with **CYNTHIA PLASTER CASTER**

Interview by Betty Boob

Want your man to stay hard forever? Call Cynthia Plaster Caster, the legendary connoisseur of casting cock. As part of our bad girls issue, **BUST** *sat down with the High Priestess of Penis, who regaled us with colorful stories of life on her knees.* **What's the story of Cynthia Plaster Caster?** My girlfriend Pest and I really liked British rock musicians; we liked their hair, the way they wore tight pants and we could see these bulges that were, to me, a source of mystery, because I had never seen a dick. So I was an art major and my art teacher said, "Make a plaster cast. Pick an object that can retain it's shape, that's kind of on the hard side," and I'm thinking, OMIGOD! I knew *exactly* what I wanted to cast. Pest and I went to hunt down bands that weekend. The Hollies were in town for a show and I think Herb Alpert and the Tijuana Brass. Most of them were staying at the Hilton. We knocked on Billy Joe Royal's door and said, "Hey, we'd like to make a plaster cast of your rig" [British slang for penis]. He whipped out his semi-hard-on, kind of waving it in the wind! We thought, well, that was a good response. **What was your first successful time like?** Well it was Jimi Hendrix. I was nervous. **So you meet Jimi and what does he say to you?** It was after a show in Chicago. We pulled up to the Hilton and said "Hi Jimi, we're the Plaster Casters" and he was like "Oh yeah yeah yeah, I've heard about you, come up to my room and let's do it!" I was using breathing control to try to hide the fact that I was

page design: Laurie Henzel

very much freaking. When my mold was ready my friend Diane gave him a blow job and then he dipped. But I forgot to lubricate his pubes. Somehow I forgot! I don't remember having pube problems with the two friends I'd done [for practice]. Jimi's pubes were dry and as a result they got stuck in the mold. That's the only part of the genitals that has to be oiled. By the time the mold hardens the dick is usually soft enough to kind of slide out, but hair is really tricky. I had to pull out one hair at a time to avoid him going through too much pain.

I have to ask, is Jimi's the biggest?
It's the thickest but not the longest. I would have to take a wild guess and say Clint from Pop Will Eat Itself is the longest; but his is twisted. Sometimes they come out curled, like snakes or pigs' tails.

How long does the dick have to be hard once it's inside the alginate?
They only have to be hard for anywhere from forty seconds to a minute and twenty seconds.

How many casts do you have?
I've made about fifty attempts but have only succeeded in maybe thirty-five and five-eighths. I say fractions because sometimes I only capture the head or half of the shaft or a third of the shaft with head.

I wanna know more about some of the dicks you've casted. I'm gonna throw out some names, okay? The Mekons.
Yeah. John Langford. Long John they call him.

Wow, is he that big?
Yeah. He is such a wonderful person. I love it when nice guys have big dicks.

Kurt Cobain?
I happened to be present at the Crash Palace in Chicago, this trendy bar where Nirvana went after their show and Courtney Love turned up there. Courtney introduced us and I asked Kurt if he would be interested in posing for me. He said, well you can cast my middle finger because it's representative of how I feel about the music industry. That was the night they consummated their love.

Chris Connelly [of the Revolting Cocks and Ministry]?
He was one of the singers, now he's a singer solo artist. Great guy, great cock, very talented singer-songwriter.

What do you mean, "great cock"?
Vaginal size. It's above-average size, not too thin, not too long. I have tried casting him four times. His dick is like a Bermuda Triangle—the mold failed each time! I'm talking about different days where I don't mix fast enough or the water temperature is too warm. He's been so nice and sweet and patient.

Who else is on the Cynthia P. Caster hit list?
All of them! They're all eligible. Anytime I utter the name of somebody I'm going to do, it never happens—it's the curse of the caster.

So, what is dick?
What is dick? Oh, it's that magical, mysterious, cute, very unintimidating thing in the sky. It's much funnier looking than I expected it to be. I thought that it would be some hot dog-looking shape, I didn't know there would be a head on it and balls. The shape of it is kind of clown-like and that's what I like about it. It's almost like some toy saying "Please eat me, want me, love me!" Not a scary object at all.

This Ain't No Fucking Zoo

Aaron launched **COMETBUS** *in 1981, just after he turned thirteen, as a way to plug into punk music. It has since evolved to include interviews, essays, travelogues, and short stories. Cometbus is nothing fancy, just the observations and opinions of a talented storyteller, presented in Aaron's distinctive lettering.*

EVERYONE WAS FRIENDLY IN THE RAIN. I'D GO DOWNTOWN AND SIT AROUND ALL DAY BY MYSELF JUST WATCHING THE BUILDINGS AND OCCASIONALLY MEETING SOMEONE ELSE PRETENDING TO BE ANTI-SOCIAL. ONE GUY NAMED COACH EXPLAINED HOW EVERYTHING IN LIFE RELATED TO STAR TREK. ANOTHER GUY TRADED HIS MAG FOR ONE OF MINE. HIS WAS A DETAILED PLAN OF EXACTLY WHAT WE NEEDED TO TAKE WITH US IN THE SPACESHIPS WHEN IT WAS TIME TO ABANDON EARTH. I BROUGHT IT BACK TO THE ATTIC AND STUDIED IT AND TOOK SOME NOTES. WHEN I SAW THE GUY AGAIN I TOLD HIM I LIKED HIS PLAN EXCEPT FOR A FEW THINGS. MELTING DOWN THE WEIGHT LIFTING EQUIPMENT AND TURNING IT INTO FARMING TOOLS ONCE WE GOT TO A NEW PLANET, THAT WAS A GOOD IDEA. BUT COCA LEAVES AND PARSNIPS INSTEAD OF, SAY, PENICILLIN AND WHEAT, WAS A BAD IDEA. HE JUST STOOD THERE IN SHOCK, NODDING IN AGREEMENT. I WAS OBVIOUSLY THE FIRST PERSON TO READ HIS PLAN AND RETURN TO DISCUSS THE FINE POINTS.

SLUGGO LIVED IN A SQUAT RIGHT BY DOWNTOWN, AND SOMETIMES

ZINE VOICES

"I think I started self-publishing because people wouldn't listen to me. I don't know if it's because I'm a girl or if I just have a soft, uncommanding voice. But I found that people would listen if I wrote it down and published it. By sending you this zine, I have you by the collar for at least 20 minutes!"

—Julee Peezlee, *McJob*

I'D DUCK IN THERE TO ESCAPE THE RAIN, AND ATTEMPT TO GET SOME WRITING DONE. THE HIDDEN BACK DOOR LED TO THE FIRST FLOOR, WHICH WAS VACANT. THE TRAPDOOR LED TO THE SECOND FLOOR WHICH WAS OCCUPIED BY PISSBUCKETS AND THE PIGEONS WHO STARED AT YOU WHILE YOU PEED. THE STAIRS LED TO THE THIRD FLOOR, WHERE SLUGGO AND SAL LIVED. THE HOUSE HAD BEEN PARTLY DESTROYED BY A FIRE, THEN PARTLY REMODELED, AND NOW TOTALLY ABANDONED FOR QUITE SOME TIME. SLUGGO AND SAL HAD FIXED IT UP SO BEAUTIFULLY, BUILDING A KITCHEN, PUTTING UP PICTURES, PAINTING MURALS. GIVE THEM A NICE HOME AND THEY WOULD TRASH IT, REDUCE IT TO RUBBLE. BUT GIVE THEM RUBBLE AND TRASH, AND THEY HAD TURNED IT INTO ONE OF THE NICEST, COOLEST, MOST BEAUTIFUL HOMES I HAD EVER SEEN.

ONE DAY I WAS AT THE SQUAT WITH SLUGGO, AND WE WERE TRYING TO WRITE. WE SAT IN THE SUNNIEST ROOM, THE ONE WITH THE SKYLIGHT, AND SPREAD OUR NOTES EVERYWHERE. I WAS SICK AND FEVERISH FROM SITTING IN THE RAIN TOO MUCH. WE BOTH FELT LIKE HELL. SLUGGO DECIDED TO GO OUT TO TRY TO FIND THE CRACKHEAD WHO STOLE HIS BIKE. I SAT ALONE IN THE SQUAT, WRAPPED UP IN BLANKETS, DRINKING TEA AND CROSSING OFF LINES AND CRUMPLING UP PAPER. I LOOKED OUT THE WINDOW AND SAW SOMETHING ON THE BACK DECK. IT WAS A PEACOCK. THEN TWO PEACOCKS. I CHEWED MY NAILS AND MADE FUNNY WORRIED FACES, LOOKING AROUND THE ROOM HOPING SOMEONE ELSE COULD CONFIRM WHAT WAS HAPPENING. BUT NO ONE ELSE WAS HOME. I STARED AT THE PEACOCKS IN DISBELIEF, AND THEY STARED BACK AT ME. IT WAS WEIRD ENOUGH THAT PEACOCKS WERE WANDERING AROUND, BUT IT WAS TOO STRANGE THAT THEY WERE ON THE DECK, THREE FLOORS UP, STARING AT ME. IN FACT, PEACOCKS WERE THE WORST THING THAT COULD POSSIBLY SHOW UP AT A SQUAT. SLUGGO AND SAL HAD TAKEN EVERY PRECAUTION TO REMAIN DISCREET AND SECRETIVE ABOUT LIVING THERE, AND NOW THERE WERE PEACOCKS ON THE PORCH.

I FIGURED MAYBE THEY WERE JUST THIRSTY, SO I FILLED UP A DISH OF WATER. I OPENED THE BACK DOOR QUIETLY SO AS NOT TO SCARE THEM OFF. THE PEACOCKS WERE NOT SCARED. THEY CHARGED TOWARDS ME SQUAWKING, TRYING TO GET IN THE DOOR. I JUMPED BACK INSIDE AND BARRICADED THE DOOR. I TRIED TO IGNORE THEM AS THEY BANGED ON THE WINDOWS. IT IS HARD TO WRITE WHILE IGNORING PEACOCKS. I LOOKED AROUND AND LAUGHED. I KNEW SLUGGO WOULD NEVER BELIEVE ME WHEN HE GOT HOME.

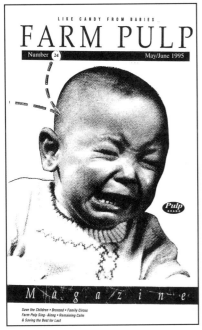

LIKE CANDY FROM BABIES

FARM PULP

Number 24   May/June 1995

Pulp BRAND

M a g a z i n e

Save the Children • Bronzed • Family Circus
Farm Pulp Sing - Along • Remaining Calm
& Saving the Best for Last

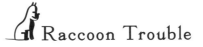 Raccoon Trouble

Gregory Hischak's zine, **FARM PULP**, *contains more folds than a road map, making it as much fun to unwrap as to read. Launched in 1990 when a lonely photocopier at work cried out for attention,* Farm Pulp *returned for a second issue, and eventually a twenty-seventh, because "it's cheaper than therapy, more stable than a girlfriend, and less demanding than religion," as Gregory puts it. His research for the following selection consisted of using a dictionary to look up the Latin classification for raccoons. The story is true.*

I broke up with my girlfriend and spent a lot of time around the house dealing with it. My house seemed a secure haven in which to lick my wounds and in the quiet darkness of my bedroom I watched science fiction serials with the volume off and began the healing process.

One night I was awakened by a crash in the yard. Garbage can to gravel. I immediately thought to myself: *Raccoons.* I put on my robe. Out in the hall, Little Cooling Tower wagged her tail worriedly and looked toward the back door with a *Do you know there are raccoons out there?* expression.

I went outside. Sure enough, the garbage had been overturned and jagged shards of Styrofoam container—beef and bean burrito—littered the porch. Grumbling, I collected the mess and shut the lid down on the can loudly, placing a brick on top. I had walked no more than three steps back into the house when there was the crash of a brick splintering the door. I ran out quickly and saw the same brick I had just placed on the garbage can. I looked into the bushes and heard the rapid hissing of two creatures, as if they were snickering.

I seemed to be having a raccoon problem.

This wasn't my first encounter with raccoons. A summer of camping had taught me that not only can they climb trees, tightrope across lines, undo zippers, and unscrew bottles, raccoons could also break into trunks, steal change, and take library books out in your name and not return them.

Hardly a long lonely night went by without them rummaging through my garbage. Every night, I listened to their conspiring murmurs like uninvited guests at a wedding reception. I heard their dexterous procyonid feet across my gravel. I cringed as the outside faucet came on and they hosed down some pilfered morsel.

That was the worst part, that they washed everything they ate. Not only stealing my food, but helping themselves to my water as well. I lie in bed looking at the television until just before dawn, when the raccoons rapped goodnight against the window and I would get dressed for work.

Attempting to starve them out, I ate out frequently but this was complicated by the fact I no longer had a girlfriend. I found it torturous dining out alone. I became tortured by the possibility

I might bump into her. So instead, I ate frugally at home. What I couldn't finish I force-fed to Little Cooling Tower.

Working in my garden, I noticed produce disappearing. One day the corn vanished. An apple tree was picked clean. Of my carrot crop only three plants remained—pulling one up, I found a raccoon attached to it, devouring it from the bottom. He scowled at me with those black bandit eyes and tugged the plant violently out of my hand before disappearing back into the hole.

While I suspected they spent their days asleep, they began to become more daring. One morning they pulled out my lawn furniture and sunned themselves on the porch. Returning home I would find the concrete littered with cigarette butts and Little Cooling Tower in the kitchen, sheepishly washing out their glasses.

I caught raccoons sleeping in the back seat of my car. I haven't a clue how they got the door unlocked. I was always low on gas. Were the raccoons joy riding or merely siphoning the tank? I had dead bolts installed. I canceled my credit cards. I had my mail forwarded to a post office box. I had no idea what they were capable of doing.

Though I am by nature nonviolent, desperation forced me to lay traps. I sat inside that night and listened through the window. I heard what sounded like a large crowd of ruffians playing with my garden hose. They were washing down their evening meal. I heard what I assumed to be beer cans popping open. Later I heard one of them playing guitar and the raspy hissing chuckle of a joke shared at someone's expense.

The next morning every single trap I placed had been piled up against the front door. Beyond them, the sidewalk was covered with wet handfuls of white fur. A plastic deli bag was left near the gate—inside what seemed to be the bones of a small animal (picked clean) and Little Cooling Tower's green collar.

I was *really* having raccoon problems.

I called the city. "Sure," the strangely familiar voice said, "*We'll be tendin' tomeone ovah deyeh.*" And then, as though muffled through a furry clawed hand, I heard the voice say across the room: "Ah tol' him we'd be tendin' tomeone ovah deyeh." I slammed the phone down.

Panicked, I ran up the street to a bar. The place was crowded and noisy. I began to relax in the camaraderie that comes when one is surrounded by one's own species. I glanced over at a corner booth and, my worst fears realized, spotted my ex-girlfriend. She was in a booth near the back and sitting across from her was one of *them*. She was *sitting there* with this raccoon. A hulking dull looking grayish brute who wolfishly leaned over the table lighting her cigarette. He must be twice her age, I thought, watching him dexterously manipulate the child-proof lighter with his long dark claws.

I quickly walked outside and narrowly missed being struck by my own car. Two squat, dirty gray raccoons waved back at me from the front seat before accelerating sharply into a curve. They were joy riding and out for blood. They had *meant* to hit me.

It was dark by the time I arrived home. I locked every bolt in the house and lay in bed for hours in a cold sweat, startled by every snapping twig, every click and whirl that fills a dark house when you lie there and listen for them. Around four o'clock I recognized the sound of my car pulling up. It crunched against the gravel and then stopped. I counted the clicks of sixteen pairs of clawed feet. Were there four of them, or were they walking erect, making sixteen? It was hard to tell.

Terror pounded blood through my head, making it hard to distinguish the sounds: Metallic. Clinking. Something dropped. Something retrieved and finally the heaving groan of the front door. They had keys made! *Raccoons knew how to have keys made!* I grabbed the phone in the dark, madly punching 911. Over the headpiece I heard another low, raspy voice giving someone, *something*, directions to my house. They were on my kitchen phone.

Down the hall, the bathroom light flashed on, silhouetting two raccoons against my bedroom door. They were standing erect. *Procyon lotors standing erect!* I heard the clattering of dishes and splashing from the bathtub as a sinewy hand covered my mouth. Or was it a foot? Another pair of appendages grabbed my wrists and began dragging me down the hall to where a tub of cold water would, for *their* purposes, do nicely.

All I could think of while being pulled violently down my own hallway to be ceremoniously washed in my own tub before my own certain slaughter was that I *really* had a raccoon problem now. It was my problem and on some level or another, I was going to have to deal with it.

porn

☝ Schmeckel Movies in California

Dick Freeman's monthly zine, **BATTERIES NOT INCLUDED**, *reviews and celebrates porn movies as healthy, erotic diversions. It's fascinating and funny and sometimes obscene, but that's a compliment. One of my favorite contributors is Richard Pacheco, a former adult-film star who occasionally submits chapters of his autobiography and even cost Dick a radio host gig once after he read an essay on the air called "My Last Cum Shot." Lovely. Reading Richard's account of being outed, reprinted here from BNI's second issue, I can only hope my mother would have the same reaction.*

You know what a schmeckel is, don't you? Sure you do. A schmeckel is a schmuck, a dick, a cock, a man's thingee, a penis in the dictionary, and a body part of mine that has figured prominently in my former semi-adult choice of professions. That understood, let me tell you a little story.

The telephone was ringing. I was drunk, on my way home from a wedding reception. After finally managing to turn the key in the lock, I rushed inside.

"Hello?" I was breathless.

"You're busted!" came a hard, raspy voice.

It's amazing how fast those two words can sober you up. Then I caught myself. I recognized the voice.

"Is this Bennie?"

"Yeah," said Bennie, "and you're busted!" My cousin Bennie lived in Pittsburgh, where we had grown up.

"What are you talking about, Bennie? What happened?"

"Cousin Marvin saw you in a porno film!"

Marvin was a high-priced lawyer in Washington, D.C., for the company that made Valium. Marvin had skipped work one afternoon from his fancy schmancy office to treat himself to a dirty movie. Just my luck, it was *The Candy Stripers*, my first film. I earned $200 for getting a blow job in a closet. The scene took eight hours to film, but that's really another story.

The point here is that Cousin Marvin thought he recognized me in the movie. He got so excited that he drove home to Maryland, picked up his wife in Suburbia, left their kids with the neighbors, and drove back into D.C. to show Cousin Naomi the movie. After watching the scene, Naomi confirmed it was me.

Marvin became so excited that he didn't know what to do with himself. He called my mother. He was going to tell on me. I was thirty-two years old, also married with kids. I hadn't lived at home in fourteen years. Marvin was thirty-seven.

My mother wasn't home, so Marvin called *his* mom, my Aunt Sylvia. Horrified, she made him promise not to tell my mother. It seems that Sylvia had once taken her to see the film *Last Tango in Paris*. When Marlon Brando started buttering up Maria Schneider's ass, my mother dragged Sylvia out of the theater.

"So, how did you find out all about this?" I asked Bennie. "Did Aunt Sylvia tell you?"

"No," Bennie said. "Aunt Tillie told me." This was getting more complicated by the minute. If Aunt Tillie and Aunt Sophie knew, then Uncle Joe and Uncle Jake must also. And that meant Aunt Sylvia's new husband, Ziggie, had heard.

"Why didn't Marvin just call me?"

"How the hell should I know? You know Marvin. He's always been a jag-off."

Before I got off the phone, I began to feel the anguish of being an embarrassment to my mother. I could picture the ugly little scene at the next bar mitzvah, with the other guests snickering behind her back. It was no good. I had to do something. Before the day was out, I would tell my mother about my X-rated career. Then I would find Cousin Marvin and punch out his ugly, Valium face.

As I dialed the number of my origin, I tried to prepare myself to become the black sheep of the family. The sexual revolution had skipped Pittsburgh, and pornography was still equated with mobsters and prostitution. I imagined the news bulletins: "Local Jewish Boy Discovered Fucking Shiksas for Cash in California." My wife got on the line for moral support.

My mother answered on the second ring. We exchanged small talk. She was readying the house for my older brother's return. After ten years in Israel, my brother the doctor was moving his family back to Pittsburgh. My mother was ecstatic.

"Listen, Ma," I said finally. "I have to tell you something."

"Yeah?"

"Yeah," I said, steeling myself. "A while back I did a couple of X-rated movies." (Actually, I had done thirty films, along with ten loops and two magazine pictorials, but I thought I'd take it slow.) "I didn't tell you because I didn't think you'd be crazy to hear about it . . ."

"Ye . . . ah . . ." my mother said haltingly. She was no dummy. She was waiting for the bomb to drop.

"Well, Cousin Marvin stumbled into one of my movies in Washington and . . ."

"He goes to those movies?!"

"I guess so, Ma," I said, relieved to put the onus on Marvin. "He got himself all excited at seeing me and called Aunt Sylvia."

"Aunt Sylvia? Why didn't he call you?"

"Good question. The bottom line is I wanted you to hear it from me before the gossip started flying."

Silence.

"What was the movie's name?" she asked.

"*The Candy Stripers* was the one Marvin saw."

"How much did they pay you?"

"I got $200 a day." It was the truth. "I worked with Marilyn Chambers," I added. That was not the truth. I had worked with Marilyn, but on another film. Somehow I thought her fame might help me legitimize the whole thing.

"Who?" my mother asked.

"Marilyn Chambers, Ma. You remember, the Ivory Snow girl? The woman with the baby?"

"You worked with a baby?"

"No, Ma. Marilyn Chambers was on the Ivory Snow package *with* the baby. Then when they found out she'd worked in a porn movie, they fired her. Remember? It was all over the papers, Ma, front page."

"Oh. So that's your news?"

"Yeah, that's my news."

"You want to know what I think?" she asked. Here it comes . . .

"Plllbbbbbbbb!" she spat. "That's what I think."

My mom gave me the raspberry! I laughed. My wife laughed. My mom laughed.

That was it!

After I hung up, I imagined my mother running into one of her friends at the kosher butcher shop.

"So, how are your kids?" the friend would ask.

"Fine," my mother would answer. "My son, the doctor, is coming back from Israel and my other son, the one in California, he's making schmeckel movies."

public service

 I'll Say Anything

Hoping to see their names in print, Mark Frauenfelder and Carla Sinclair powered up bOING bOING, their zine of techno fun, in 1988. In their first issues they tackled corsets, dead media, boorish roommates, bad typography and robot groupies, among other topics. But as circulation skyrocketed from one hundred copies to seventeen thousand, creating new material became a drag. "Our goal used to be to make bOING bOING slick and popular, but to do that we had to deal with tightwad distributors and write about stuff we weren't interested in to attract ads," explains Carla. "Now our goal is just to have fun." David Pescovitz, who conducted this interview, is a contributing editor.

The Brain Mutator for Higher Primates

bOING bOING

$3.95 number 11

The Internet: Stay for Free!
Mondo Vanilli: Satan's Pigs!
Quantum Tantra: Sticky Fun!
L.A. Vice Squad: Silly Morons!

When a deaf person wants to contact someone via telephone, they use a TT (Text Telephone)—a computer keyboard, screen, and modem—to call a free, state-supported relay service. A relay agent acts as an interpreter, reading aloud what the deaf person types to the hearing person and typing what the hearing person says for the deaf person.

Sheri, 22, was a relay agent for a year. She had to type 45 words per minute and be a very good listener.

What did you enjoy most about your job?
I was able to help people who couldn't normally communicate over the phone. It was interesting to become involved in deaf culture—being a relay agent inspired me to study sign language.

What kinds of conversations did you relay?
During the day, they were usually business calls or people ordering pizza. In the evening, the most common calls were family members talking to each other. The bizarre calls happened late at night.

Such as?
I did a few sex calls. Once, a deaf person was typing a sex call to his girlfriend. The girlfriend was hard of hearing so I had to scream for her to hear me. I was telling her things like, "I want to lick your wet pussy." All the other relay agents could hear me, so it was kind of embarrassing.

There was also a Pentecostal minister who worked at the service and he had a raunchy sex call one night. A deaf girl was typing and the minister was reading it to this hearing boyfriend. Partly because he was a minister and partly because he was a guy talking to another guy, it was pretty funny. He had to say that he wanted to touch this guy's balls. All the other agents couldn't help laughing because the minister had a really serious expression on his face. He looked like he had to concentrate pretty hard for that call.

Couldn't the woman have requested a female operator?
Yes, like if a female was calling a gynecologist for example, she may want a female relay agent. But some people didn't know they could choose or just didn't care.

Sex calls were pretty rare. But we had to do them because of the equal access policy. That means that the people who use the service can talk about whatever they want and we have to relay the conversation. The names and cities are strictly confidential. We couldn't turn a caller in, even if they were talking about something illegal.

Like drug deals?
I relayed a couple of conversations about drugs. They were usually something like "Do you have a bag of pot?"

Any other unusual calls you remember?
I had a couple of 911 calls where people reported suicidal friends. Sometimes the person calling wouldn't be a fast typist and we'd have to wait for them to respond to the 911 operator's questions. That'd make everyone a nervous wreck.

Did you ever interpret for people in arguments?
All the time. I told lots of people to "fuck off" over the phone. It was weird being in the middle of arguments. Sometimes they would ask my opinion. Like "Agent, what do you think about that? She's wrong, isn't she?" I'd say, "I'm sorry but I'm just the operator." It wasn't my job to be a counselor.

Did you talk in a monotone?
We were encouraged to use inflection so the hearing people wouldn't get completely bored. If the deaf caller typed "Fuck you, I think you're an asshole," I'd say it like I was mad.

How did you express emotion to the deaf person?
If the hearing person was laughing, I'd type in parentheses that they were laughing. If they were crying, I'd type that they were sniffling and crying. If someone was yelling, I'd use lots of exclamation points.

Did you type every word you heard?
A lot of times the hearing people would be rude and say something in the background to someone else and I would type that. Like, "I really hate getting calls from this person," or "This person is so dumb." The hearing person assumed I wouldn't type everything they said, but of course I did. That's part of equal access. If they were talking to a hearing person on the phone, they wouldn't make comments like that.

How did the hearing people react to using a relay agent?
Usually, everyone treated me like I was a robot, a machine that automatically typed and read. But every once in a while, the hearing people would get embarrassed. Like if it was a sensitive conversation about marital problems, the hearing person might say, "Let's not talk about this because of the relay agent." The deaf people wouldn't be nearly as uncomfortable because they're used to interpreters. Besides, they appreciate the relay service. Hearing people tend to think it's slow.

What was the biggest drawback to being an agent?
It got tedious sometimes, especially with long-winded people going on and on and on. Your hands would get tired.

What kind of job do you have now?
I arrange teleconference calls for a bank. I still listen in, but it's not nearly as interesting.

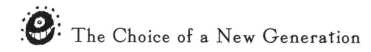

The Choice of a New Generation

Clay Butler wanted his cartoons out in the world, and what better way than to create a zine? **SIDEWALK BUBBLEGUM** *is his take on the consumer culture that consumes us all.*

revolution

The FAT!SO? Manifesto

*Marilyn Wann is fat. What's it to you? Her zine, **FAT!SO?**, written "for people who don't apologize for their size," is funny, ornery, and sexy. The extra-large issues have included cut-out dolls, flipbooks ("the incredible expanding Oprah!"), an investigation into life insurance weight tables, a series of "anatomy lessons" (such as "Butts," below) and a report from Disneyland (Thunder Mountain and the Haunted Mansion are among the roomier rides). Fat!So? makes the case that just as racial and gender differences contribute to the diversity of our society, so does size. As Marilyn likes to say, "A waist is a terrible thing to mind!"*

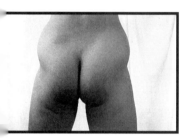 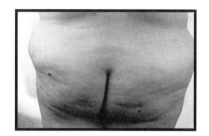 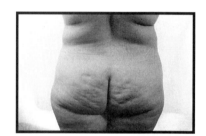

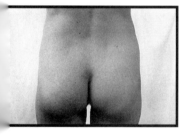 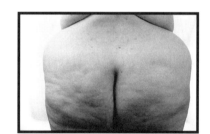 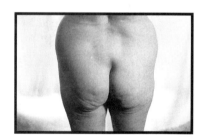

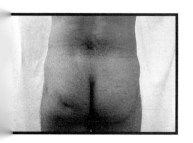 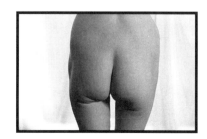 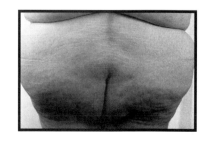

1. *FAT!SO?* calls for revolution.

The revolution starts with a simple question:

You're fat!
SO WHAT?

FAT!SO?
manifesto
BY MARILYN WANN

2. So there's nothing wrong with being fat. Just like there's nothing wrong with being short or tall, or black or brown. These are facts of identity that cannot and should not be changed. They are birthright. They're beyond aesthetics. They provide the diversity we need to survive.

3. *FAT!SO?* proclaims 12:01 a.m., January 1, 1995 The First International Fat-Outing Minute.

During this minute, round folk are called upon to stand before their mirrors and proclaim, "I am fat." The zealous will then gaze deeply into the eyes of their round loved ones and say, "You are fat, too!" Then, fatso's everywhere will applaud and blow noisemakers for a second time in as many minutes. Instead of starting the New Year with yet another resolution to lose weight on some harmful, ineffectual diet, we'll begin the last half-decade of the 20th Century with an honest moment and some relief from anxiety.

5.

FAT!SO? invites YOU
to be a fabulous fatso!

Everybody: Size 6 to 16. Size 26 to 56. Because fat or thin, straight or gay, male or female, we have all at some point wasted our precious moments on the planet worrying about how we look. Fuck that! Just say the magic words: "Yes, I am a fatso!" Write it here in the space provided: _____

With these words, you create revolution. You turn fat hatred back on itself. As a fatso, you possess the ultimate weapon against fatphobia, body prejudice, and size oppression: fatso pride!

4.
Fat people are not, by definition, lazy or stupid. People who believe in such stereotypes, however, are.

8. List the 5 people you most admire:

_____
_____
_____
_____
_____

How many of them are fat?_____
Is this more than you expected?_____
Less than you hoped?_____
What does your admiration really mean?

7.
Large,
big-boned,
overweight,
chubby,
zaftig,
voluptuous,
Rubenesque,
plump,
and
obese
are all
synonyms
for *fear.*

6. Practice saying the word *fat* until it feels the same as *short, tall, thin, young,* or *old.* Chat with your fat. Give it pet names. Doodle *fat* on your notepad during meetings: FAT fat *fat* **fat** FAT. Use it with your parents, with your partner. Let friends in on your secret. Say, "By the way, I'm fat." Not overweight, not plump, not bloated. FAT! Combine the word *fat* with other words in new and unusual ways: beautifully fat, fat and fabulous, fat pride. Use *fat* in a sentence: "You're looking good, are you getting fat?" "I met a handsome, fat man the other day." "Gee, I wish I could be fat like her." Try out these radical phrases on people you meet and watch their stunned reactions.

9. Fatphobia is a numbers game. We tell ourselves, "Oh, I could never weigh more than 140 pounds." (Or 160 pounds or 200 or more.) If you exceed this imaginary limit, your body becomes an impossibility. When I weighed 160 pounds, I thought I was too fat for words. Then I went up to 200; the unthinkable had happened. Now that I am 250 pounds and have friends twice my size, I realize this numbers game is no different from the flat world theory: We set weight horizons beyond which we expect to fall off the face of the earth. But the world is round, and all bodies are possible, acceptable, real.

10. *FAT!SO?* calls on all people everywhere to stop lying about their weight! Especially on driver's licenses! This comforting practice reinforces fatphobia and hinders size acceptance. When Gloria Steinem turned 40, people kept telling her she didn't look it. She replied: No, this is what 40 looks like. Women have lied about age for so long, we think 40 looks 32 and 32 looks 28. Likewise, people have been lying about their weight for so long that we don't know a goodlooking 250-pound person when we see one. So what? So fat people can't get jobs, lovers, health insurance, respect, etc., because our society can't imagine people weighing more than the numbers on some bogus actuarial table. Practice honesty right now! Fill in the blanks! My name is: _____
I weigh _____ pounds.

11. Fatso's, it's time we refused to be weighed during doctor visits! If a health professional pressures you to get on the scale, ask what possible medical purpose it would serve. A nurse told me, "Well, we need to track your weight so that, if it changes a lot from one visit to the next, we'll know, because it can indicate disease." Like I wouldn't notice a sudden loss of 50 pounds! Call the doctor's scale what it is: a tool of intimidation and humiliation, a means to justify the medical industry's anti-fat bias.

12. This is how we see: thin, vertical bodies are good; horizontal fat rolls are bad. A hierarchy of Y-axis over X. Marx says: reverse the terms, put fat on top. I say: dichotomies are dumb. Love it all.

rock & roll

 What Do You Know about the Beatles?

In 1979, while working at the Duplex Nursing Home in Boston, David Greenberger began asking the residents questions such as "What is instant gratification?," "When was the last time you rode a bicycle?," and "What invention would you like to improve?" He's since filled more than 145 issues of his zine, **THE DUPLEX PLANET**, *with their entertaining and enlightening responses. "The elderly aren't from another planet," David points out. "They were just born sooner."*

Bill Niemi: They were a musical organization. They're still playin', aren't they? They were in Hollywood for a while making pictures. It was on television that one of them was murdered in New York, that John Lennon. They'll probably have to reorganize the whole dance band.

Ken Eglin: Now, you know this, I don't have to tell you this: John and Paul McCarty, they never got along. Always fighting. And John told Paul, "You're never goin' anywhere!" Why he said it, I do not know. But Ringo, he didn't like the way those other two were acting. He stayed with the group though, but he had plans. Finally he got an offer to go to Hollywood and make pictures and he grabbed it. You know the rest with Ringo, now he's a movie actor. Paul I guess is making records. Oh yeah, he's makin' records, but not too many. From what I heard on television, they may start up again, come back together again. There'll be somebody in John's place. He wasn't that popular with the girls anyway. Especially after he married that Japanese girl. I didn't think too much of that, but to each his own.

Andy Legrice: They're good singers. They're good Americans.

Henry Turner: All I have to say about the Beatles is they sing too loud. To be honest with you I think they should be arrested for disturbing the peace.

Larry Green: The Beatles were good singers. They're a good quartet. "Apple Blossom Time," "God Bless America"—Kate Smith sang that, she sang it way down yonder in New Orleans. God bless America, land of the free, stand beside us and guide us—I forget all the words.

(What did the Beatles look like?) Oh geez, they was elderly. I don't know, it's been a long time since I've seen 'em. *(What were the Beatles' names?)* Larry, Moe, and Joe—the Beatles! One got shot, didn't he? *(Yes.)* Oh, Jesus, that's tough. Was it a fight over a girl? *(No.)* What was it, gamblin'? Crap game? Card game? Poker? *(No, it was just someone crazy.)* Ohhh, that's too bad. They were good. Did you ever hear the Mills Brothers?

John Lowthers: I can't tell you about the Beatles—I don't know a thing about them. I never worked for them and they never worked for me.

Edna Hemion: Oh, I can't remember that far back! I used to go to musicals in New York. There's no place like New York—my father said that and his daughter says it now.

Frank Wisnewski: Yeah, yeah, yeah, yeah, yeah, yeah! I was one of their fans. Ringo! They're all dead I think. What, was there five of them? They're all gone.

Herbie Caldwell: I don't know much about the Beatles. They chirp and play around.

Wally Baker: They started in England and toured the United States and one got bumped off. Anything else you want to know? *(Tell me about their music.)*
(Puts his hands up.) That's as far as I go.

Chuck Berry: Rocker, Legend, Landlord

After interviewing rockabilly singer Sleepy LaBeef for a punk zine that never came to be, Jake Austen began his own. Thus spake **ROCTOBER**. *"There's a theory that many zine editors work with," explains Jake. "At some point, everyone you know will tell you a great story that fits in with your theme." Skippy Lange's interview with a former Chuck Berry tenant is a case in point: After Jake asked him to write it up for the "Close Encounters of the Rockin' Kind" issue, Skippy filled fifty sheets of looseleaf paper. Other hits include Jake's fond tributes to monkeys, midgets, and masks in rock 'n' roll, an obsessive cataloging of Sammy Davis Jr. memorabilia, and a brutally honest review policy: "Everything we receive gets written up, but it gets written up by an asshole."*

If you ever find yourself lost in Hollywood (and who hasn't?), you may one day affix your gaze on a Moorish-style mansion anchored on its own circular island of rolling lawn. This is Hollyridge, the former digs of Chuck Berry. For seventeen years its tennis court was loveless, and its rooms were filled only with echo. Then a pair of enterprising lovers, John and Lee, conspired to make the place their own. The following is an account of that time by John, a man now separated from Hollyridge (he and Lee broke up) but still haunted by its song and the man who made it sing.

Skippy: So, how did you find the house?

John: Lee and I were looking for a pad, and we turn onto Bronson and see this huge house. So we pull up and met Anita, the lady who lives across the street. And she says, "Oh, that's Chuck's Hollywood mansion! Let's see if you can rent the place. We'd like to have some young people in the neighborhood." So we got Chuck on the phone, but that was very strange, y'know, the communication's barely there.

S: You mean the technology?

J: No, he wouldn't answer any questions. He'd only say, "Uh huh. Well, fax me." So after like $250 in faxes and phone calls, we finally get the contract and rent the place. Then we get a call from a neighbor who says that Chuck's coming into town and wants to meet us! So we're playing tennis on the courts at Hollyridge and this Lincoln Town Car comes around the corner. This guy hops out in this bright blue suit and I say, "There's Chuck!"

S: This is when you had all the instruments in the living room, right?

J: They were all over the place. Chuck leans his head into the bay windows and says, "Ahhh, a musician! I like that!" The guy speaks eloquently. There's like a twinge, a Southern kind of tone. And he says to me, "Well, I'm glad to see you're so tall." It just blew my mind. I didn't understand it, I don't know . . .

S: Tall in the saddle.

J: I guess. He started walking around the house and telling us about all the parties he used to have, and all the girls, and diving off the balconies into the swimming pool.

S: When did he live there?

J: He moved out of the place in 1972—lived there for eighteen months.

S: Why did he move?

J: His wife didn't like the house, and to her Hollywood was Babylon. When he left, he turned on the fireplace, which had a gas element in it, and let it burn for seven years.

S: An eternal flame.

J: Exactly. He made reference to that. So after a few hours, he invites us to his show in Orange County. We're following him in the car and he drives like you wouldn't believe—he's clocking 80 miles an hour, we're laughing like, "This is so much fun!" We go into the V.I.P. entrance, and there are sheriff's deputies all over the place, and they load us all into this trailer and start feeding us chicken. Chuck cracks open his case, and inside is a guitar that looks like it hasn't been played in about ten years. It has broken strings, broken pick up, broken neck. Chuck says to me, "John, go get the promoter and tell him the airlines busted my guitar." And the show is about to start! And then I'm thinking of that movie, *Hail Hail, Rock 'n' Roll*, where Chuck says he gets a new guitar every time he plays.

S: How'd the show go?

J: Oh, it was great! He tore it up, and everything was beautiful. Afterward we headed back to the mansion and he goes off to his hotel. The next morning he shows up at 10 o'clock with a ladder and a hammer and a bucket of tar and says, "Let's patch the roof!" I rub the sleep out of my eyes and we're going up ladders and he's telling me about his dad the roofer. It was a blast! I couldn't believe I was patching the roof with Chuck Berry.

So we work until midnight! The whole time he dangles this Chinese dinner in my face. "Let's go out for Chinese, on me." Nine o'clock rolls around. I say, "Chuck, we better eat." He responds, "Oh, it's too late now. How about Wendy's hamburgers?" So I wait for him to cough up the dough but he never does. I say, "I guess I'll find some money so I can get the hamburgers, Chuck." Doesn't faze him. It's 10:30 now, and he's revitalized, running around with a tape measure. I get a little irritated, so I take my meal upstairs and Lee and our roommates Alicia and Tom are hiding up there! I'm the only one left to deal with Chuck. And he's at the stairs yelling, "John! Hey! Let's get this show on the road!"

S: Johnny B. Goode!

J: Yeah! I don't believe this guy is of this earth. I never saw him eat food. He wrapped up his Wendy's hamburger and put it in his car. Once we went down to the store to get muriatic acid. Chuck pours it into this pump, hops down into the pool, and starts spraying this acid, which on contact makes you dizzy and makes your mouth water and your stomach jam and your head pound. He is engulfed with acid and he's not even winking. He's smiling! And I'm there with a rag over my mouth, wheezing, dropped to my knees. He's telling me, "Go on John, get your little young lungs out of here."

S: So instead of Superman looking like Christopher Reeve, he actually looks like Chuck Berry.

J: Yes. Chuck Berry is Superman.

KISS Memories

"Mommy and I are one" was a soothing subliminal message used by Freudian psychologists in the sixties, but there's nothing subtle about the zine of the same name. Edited by Jessica Hundley and Andy Hunter, it contains loads of music, comics, and stories plus stuff like an interview with a hard workin' Manhattan Tupperware Lady, an essay entitled "The Rise of Human Consciousness After the Fall of Man," record reviews (of course), and an insider report from someone who went to high school with someone who ended up playing a hunky character on 90210. Says Jessica of her KISS experience, which she detailed in the first issue of MOMMY AND I ARE ONE, *"It was one of the most perfect, beautifully orchestrated moments of my life."*

I'm not ashamed to admit it: I wanted KISS on the cover because I know it's a magic word—a word that draws curious hands to the magazine because of the visions, the dreams, the pained cry of a guitar, the smell of sex and hellfire. I for one still believe in KISS.

I'm in Los Angeles, first night on the mythic west coast. I'm exhausted, limp, just driven eight hours from the Grand Canyon through the Mojave desert in the dead center of August with no air conditioning. I and my fellow travelers are, however, troopers, and after peeling off a thick layer of road scum we insist on participating in L.A.'s famous nightlife. Club of choice: The Rainbow, rocker house of sin. The whole scene is hilarious—biggest goddamn heads of hair that side of the Mississippi and more muscle shirts than I can shake a stick at, and it's hoppin' and filled to the brim with flexing biceps and the slow fizz of Aquanet. Full of no-rhythm-desperate-to-get-some white kids—I'm loving it—PURE L.A. SHITHOLE ROCKERS! But in the back of my mind I'm thinking, "Where are the STAARS! I wanna see some STAARS!"

So here it is—standing outside the club and some gorilla steps on John's foot, right on the tip of the toe. John leans over (knowing my fanaticism) and whispers, "Holy shit, I think that was Gene Simmons. Act casual, go find out if it's him." So I slide around to take a good long look and hot diggity dog—it is him!—it's GENE FUCKING SIMMONS all gnarled and ashy and old, about eight-and-a-half-feet tall and dressed entirely in black, giant silver cross around no neck to speak of and these big-ass biker boots with skulls. It was unreal, more than I could have dreamed of, I'm shaking uncontrollably as he walks by me like he owns the pavement.

I follow him with my eyes (can't stop staring) and he leads me past a sign, a sign that says, "Don't miss it—KISS ALIVE—KISS cover band Rocks Hard!" and I know it's more than a sign, it's a SIGN—I mean, like a sign from the Gods, dropped down from Olympus, sewn by the Fates, a message for my soul, and I know where I'LL be Sunday 10 P.M.

And that's exactly where I was. Standing smack dab in the middle of the Roxy sold-out show, everyone around me breathless. The lights go dim and in one swift scream from the mike, we are THERE (circa 1978) drenched in nostalgia and greasepaint. They are dressed to the nines in sorry-looking real-imitation KISS costumes and makeup. Everything is there—nothing amiss—the fire, the explosions, the tongue.

And that's not all. At some point, at the height of the angst, there is movement, disturbance up in the back where the tables are (drink minimum $15). People are shouting, shoving, and the word floats like blue lightning through the crowd. THEY are here—Gene and Paul both—live in the flesh and true to the heart, the genuine article.

I glimpse through the layers of smoke—surrounded by half-naked, half-their-age females, smiling and smug as they ought to be and suddenly I am struck dumb by the beauty of it, I mean, this is the pinnacle of masturbatory actions—these men are staring at caricatures of their past selves, steeping in secondhand adoration, the ultimate stroke of the ego. My mind quivers with the psychological/social ramifications.

And somehow, somehow THE WORD has drifted up to the stage where the pseudo Gene Simmons has dropped his battle ax and is peering blindly into the crowd. I see a tear in his eye, taste salt on his lips as he opens his mouth and shouts (this is true) "This next song is dedicated to the king of rock 'n' roll"—his voice is cracked, shaking—"and I'm not talking about Elvis—I'm talking about MR. GENE SIMMONS!" The crowd moves forward in a great THROB of ecstasy, something burns in my heart and in the next cool moment I can taste the salt on my own lips.

romance

 ## Mr. Score and His Coat of Love

To devoted readers of Russ Forster's zine, **8-TRACK MIND**, *8-tracks are more than a hobby. They're a lifestyle. Each issue offers history lessons, rare track sightings ("Never Mind the Bollocks" has sold for a hundred bucks), and letters from readers overjoyed to find others who share their love of kerchunk. In this article from a 1991 issue, Dan Sutherland (the cameraman for Russ' 8-track documentary, "So Wrong They're Right") recalls an early experience with the format.*

High school in Muskegon, Michigan, circa 1972 was not the happiest time. I took my social role with the crowd of geeks and onanists. Despite our distrust of ideals, we sought a role model to elevate our self-esteem. We needed—in order to avoid our fear of the draft and the town's iron foundries—a legitimate icon to lift us above the horse latitudes of chronic teenage depression.

Gary Sole became our beacon.

He wasn't much to look at. He was thin and tall, with a septic cough from smoking cork-filtered Kools. Extensive acne made his unerupted skin resemble smoked cheese. His hair was maintained with a Sears home barber kit and a portable trim comb. He had somehow gotten a pair of safety glasses with purple lenses, one of which had broken and was held in place with bits of duct tape and thin copper wire.

All of this wouldn't normally add up to a sex machine. But Gary's genius lay in invention. He ransacked his father's inventory of Korean War uniforms for an extra-large raincoat. Then he combed Goodwill for fur pelts and

velvet remnants, which he stitched to form a plush lining. Next he reworked the inner pockets using waterproof fisherman's bags. In the right pocket he wired two (2) six-volt batteries in series. In the left he placed a Kraco stereo 8-track player. In the loose material below the arms he rigged speakers. The remaining pocket space was dedicated to a revolving collection of 8-track tapes.

He was ready to be the leader of demi-men.

Gary never went after young women who had clean hair and print work figures. I remember him saying, as if it were yesterday, "Why should I waste my time on her? She wants Joe College. Mister Smoothie with a cool car. I don't even have a ride. There's a lot more fish in the sea. And one who'll be nice to me. Know what I mean?"

As I remember him telling it, his usual score routine went like this: "I meet a chick. Walk with her. And I'm nice. No swearing, no bragging, no talking about anyone else but her. The music is playing. Soft stuff, nice stuff. Sensitive, you know. Like Jim Croce, the Carpenters, Carole King, maybe Cat Stevens. No R&B. Make-out music.

"Then I show her the coat. She's impressed and says things like, 'Wow, you can sew, too. Never met a guy who could sew.' She reaches out and touches the lining. You know, actually has her hands move over the sable and the fox. And I tell her what the furs are and how much they're worth. They love to stroke it. Then I ask if she's ever been on a fur skin blanket before. And if she's tired and all. I time it so it all starts to happen when we're near the woods by the golf course or the cemetery.

"If my timing is right, the tape starts to repeat itself when we're in the woods and I'm identifying the wildflowers to her. I say something like, 'Your turn to choose a tape.' They'll always pull out the Cat Stevens because the rest of the tapes are hard rock like Brownsville Station or Spooky Truth. Chicks hate that shit. They choose 'Tea for the Tillerman.' And it always breaks.

What's inside? A reel of knotted tape? No, cigarettes, matches, a joint, some change and a couple of condoms. It all falls in her lap. I act ashamed.

"Then I ask to share the joint with her. If she's pissed, that's okay. I find another soft tape that's been tucked away. There's new music, the soft coat, the joint and the bed sock. The player's great because you don't have to change it. Your hands are free."

I had to borrow that coat. My buddies said I'd have to bribe Gary with exotica like Thai Sticks, super-eight porno, or 8-tracks of his choice. But there was this girl named Juanita Switzer who lived by the paper mill. One day I sneaked up behind her and smelled her scalp and I'd been a mess of an *unter-geek* ever since. I decided to pay Mister Score a visit.

Although it was late, Gary wasn't out when I came to call. The lights were on in his basement hideaway. As I crawled up to the window, I expected to hear some smooth music. Instead, I heard a vacuum cleaner. I saw him standing by his mirror. He took the nozzle of the vacuum and placed it firmly against his neck. A minute and a half later, he pulled it away to reveal a purple oval on his skin. I was stunned. Then, with the vacuum still running, he held the nozzle with one hand as he rubbed the worn sable and fox of his coat with the other. I sensed where the scene was leading and turned away.

At school the next day Gary offered another tale of romance in the bushes. I nodded and walked away. I hadn't lost hope, but I had lost an ideal.

FREE ADVICE

"Just because you have a print run of less than one hundred doesn't mean you don't have to learn the difference between its and it's."

—Dan Kelly, *Chum*

Punk Rock Love Is . . .

This selection opened the thirtieth issue of **COMETBUS**. *Says Aaron, "It's a collection of those pure moments you remember no matter what happens the morning after."*

PUNK ROCK LOVE **IS** FUCKING BEHIND THE DUMPSTER DOWN THE STREET FROM THE SHOW. FUCKING IN THE SHOWER AT THE HOTEL CARLTON. MAKING OUT IN THE RECYCLE BIN. LOOKING AT HER TATTOOS WHILE SHE'S ASLEEP. TAKING SHOWERS TOGETHER. PLAYING CHECKERS WITH CIGARETTE BUTTS. WATCHING HER BAND PLAY. DUMPSTERING VEGGIES TOGETHER AND THEN GOING BACK TO HER PLACE AND COOKING UP A FEAST. KNOWING THE SAME PARTS OF THE SAME SONGS. BOTH OF YOU HAVING THE SAME EX-GIRLFRIEND.

PUNK ROCK LOVE **IS** HAVING TO TIE HER SHOES FOR HER CUZ SHE'S TOO DRUNK. KISSING UNDER THE OVERPASS. HER SENDING YOU HER WHOLE DIARY TO READ. HER GIVING YOU TEN ROLLS OF DUCT TAPE FOR YOUR BIRTHDAY. HER BEATING UP SKINHEADS. GOING TO THE PROM ON HER MOTORCYCLE AND CHECKING IN THE HELMETS AT THE COATCHECK. GETTING ASTONISHED STARES FROM ALL THE JOCKS WHO THOUGHT YOU WERE GAY, NOW THEY FEEL DUMB CUZ YOU'RE WITH AN OLDER PUNK ROCK BOMBSHELL AND THEY'RE WITH THEIR FRIEND'S LITTLE SISTER.

PUNK ROCK LOVE **IS** MEETING HER OUTSIDE THE CLUB AND HER SAYING COME HOME WITH ME OR I'M GONNA KICK YOUR FUCKIN ASS. GOING HOME WITH HER AND SHE ALMOST KICKS YOUR ASS ANYWAY. SHARING HAIRDYE. RIDING DOUBLE ON A BIKE. BEING LOUD AND NOT CARING. SNEAKY EYES AND SLEEVLESS T-SHIRTS. THE SUN COMING UP AND YOU REALIZING THAT THERE'S OTHER PEOPLE ON THE BEACH. A GOOD SLEAZY ONE WEEK STAND. STILL BEING FRIENDS AFTERWARDS, MOST OF THE TIME.

PUNK ROCK LOVE **IS** HER SNEAKING OUT IN THE MIDDLE OF THE NIGHT TO MEET YOU IN THE PARK. RUNNING YOUR FINGERS OVER HER SPIKEY HAIR. HER CHEWING ON A FLOWER AND YOU HAVING TO CALL POISON CONTROL WHEN HER TONGUE SWELLS UP. BRINGING HER TO THE LAUNDROMAT FOR A DATE. SHARING A SLEEPING BAG AND WAKING UP FREEZING IN THE MIDDLE OF THE NIGHT AND HER, BLEARY EYED, TRYING TO HEAT IT UP WITH A BLOWDRIER. SOCIAL UNREST PLAYING "EVER FALLEN IN LOVE?" AT THE GIG YOU'RE BOTH AT THE NIGHT

AFTER SHE DUMPS YOU HARD. STARTING SMOKING AGAIN AFTER THAT NIGHT.

PUNK ROCK LOVE IS HER DRAWING ON YOU. HER SLEEPING ON YOUR BACK. HER BEING MAD AT YOU FOR BEING SUCH A JERK. HER THINKING IT'S COOL THAT YOU STINK AND YOUR HAIR STANDS UP BY ITSELF. HER HAVING WEIRD ROOMMATES WHO WORSHIP EGGS. YOU WAITING IN THE DOORWAY FOR HOURS HOPING SHE MIGHT PASS BY. EVEN IN THE SNOW. HER SINGING ALONG WITH DESCENDENTS RECORDS OVER THE AIR ON HER LATE NIGHT RADIO SHOW. HER PICTURE ON THE FRONT PAGE OF THE MORNING PAPER, GETTING ARRESTED. HER BORROWING YOUR FAVORITE BLACK HAT AND NEVER GIVING IT BACK.

PUNK ROCK LOVE IS FINDING A GIRL WHO DRINKS AS MUCH COFFEE AS YOU DO. GOING INTO THE CAFE WHERE SHE WORKS AND SHE LOOKS UP AND SMILES AND DOESN'T NOTICE AS SHE TIPS OVER A PILE OF 50 DISHES. THEY HIT THE FLOOR ONE BY ONE AND WHEN IT'S ALL DONE EVERYONE IN THE CAFE APPLAUDS AND YOU BOTH TURN BEET RED.

PUNK ROCK LOVE IS BOTH OF YOU DOING FANZINES. YEARS LATER HER TEACHING ENGLISH TO COLLEGE FRESHMEN, YOU STILL DOING FANZINES. HER WEARING GLASSES THOUGH HER EYES ARE FINE, USING CRUTCHES THOUGH HER LEGS ARE FINE, AND TALKING WITH A FAKE SPEECH IMPEDEMENT. YOU JUST THINKING IT'S RAD GIRL STYLE, UNTIL LATER WHEN SOMEONE BRINGS UP THE CONCEPT OF SELF-IMPOSED HANDICAPS.

PUNK ROCK LOVE IS GETTING YOUR FIRST KISS AND ALMOST LOSING YOUR VIRGINITY AT THE SAME TIME, MEANWHILE YOU'RE TRYING NOT TO WAKE UP THE OTHER PERSON SLEEPING IN THE SAME BED. GROPING IN THE BUSHES BY THE FREEWAY AND LATER YOU REALIZE THAT ALL THE PASSING CARS COULD SEE YOU. EXPLORING THE WASTELAND TOGETHER. HOLDING HANDS OUT ON THE FIRE ESCAPE. LYING IN THE GRASS IN HER BACKYARD. LYING ON THE ASTROTURF IN HER BEDROOM. DRINKING TEQUILA ON HER PORCH, ON YOUR BIRTHDAY. RIDING ON HER MOTORCYCLE EARLY IN THE COLD MORNING AND YOU'RE HOLDING ON TIGHT AND STEAM IS RISING OFF OF THE RIVER AND YOU'RE THINKING HOW SHE IS MAYBE EVEN BETTER THAN THE RAMONES.

PUNK ROCK LOVE IS BOTH BEING BROKE. LOVE LETTERS. FINDING OUT SHE SANG "STAY FREE" AT HER HIGH SCHOOL TALENT SHOW. FINDING OUT SHE'S A LITTLE CRAZIER THAN YOU THOUGHT WHEN YOU FINALLY GET HER IN BED. HER BOYFRIEND GETTING MAD. WALKING AROUND WITH HER AND HER NEPHEW AND EVERYONE GIVING YOU DIRTY LOOKS CUZ THEY THINK HE'S YOUR KID. WALKING AROUND WITH HER AND BEING HAPPY AND PROUD. BEING SAD TOGETHER. BEING SAD BY YOURSELF. MISSING HER.

The Truth about Fonzie
and Mrs. C.

"There are too many magazines that treat television like trash," says Dean Williams. **TV GRIND** *hopes to change that. Dean's premiere issue included the thought-provoking "Why I Like Television Racists & Retards" ("If it wasn't supposed to be funny, why did they name him Corky?"), as well as a Viewmaster reel shot from "Bonanza" in which the cast members are each furtively flipping the bird. A later issue explored "The Big Game of the Goose" (the strangest Spanish-language game show going) and offered John Migliore's compare-and-contrast treatment of "Three's Company" and Shakespeare's* As You Like It. *This selection by John appeared in* TV Grind's *first issue.*

"Boy, when you move in, you really move in, don'tcha?"

—*Howard Cunningham, to Fonzie*

Fonzie had the hots for Marion and she felt the same. Their feelings can be traced to the beginnings of "Happy Days." What about Howard "Hey, that's my wife!" Cunningham? His role is a simple and timeless one—cuckold. Either he didn't know what was happening or he was powerless to stop it. After eleven years and 255 episodes, there was more than enough evidence to prove this shocking point.

Early Indicators

Here's one example from the first season: Howard and Marion are chaperones at a school dance. Fonzie asks Marion to dance. Howard gets stuck with a hag who falls asleep in his arms. Marion gets dipped. She hasn't lost touch with her youth—and youth hasn't lost touch with her. In an early Christmas episode Howard wants the family together for Christmas Eve. No outsiders. But Fonzie is welcomed into his home just the same.

Marion: Fonzie, you're staying here and I don't want to hear another word about it.
Fonzie: Hey, Mrs. C., my mother used to talk to me like that. She was the only person who used to get away with it too, until you. I accept your invitation.

From early on, Fonzie breaks down Howard's role as head of the household. Each time he loses, Fonzie gains more power.

Arthur and Marion

The idea of taking in a boarder is clearly Marion's. She refers to the boarder as a "him" even before anyone applies. Fonzie takes the room above the garage, which bothers Howard (like anyone cares) and delights Marion.

> "Mrs. Cunningham has special privileges. She's allowed to call Fonzie by his real name of Arthur and she's permitted to give him a kiss on the cheek. Legions of fans would like to do the same!"
>
> —*from "The Truth About Fonzie"*

It's immediately clear that Fonzie is no simple lodger—he even eats with the family. This was never Howard's plan. When Fonzie stands at the dinner table every time Marion enters the room, poor Howard must comply.

Clearly, Marion fills the qualifications of a good wife better than any of Fonzie's semi-steady girlfriends. During one episode, Fonzie wants to marry a girl but Howard reveals that she is a stripper (which clashes with Fonzie's "must be untried" rule). Howard seems to know a lot about strippers.

Howard always seems to do the wrong thing, which pushes Marion closer to Fonzie. Once Marion wanted Howard to dance with her in a contest. Howard laughs and turns her down. Marion then asks Fonzie, who graciously accepts. They practice every morning at Arnold's and again after work at Fonzie's garage. Of course, everyone suspects that they're fooling around.

Ralph: We found out about you and Mrs. C. fooling around with the neighbor's wife! Bad, Fonz, bad!
Potsie: Yeah, Fonz! Bad!

A number of other characters, including Arnold, Howard, Richie and Joanie, come to the same conclusion. When they are "discovered," Marion wants to back out of the contest, but Fonzie insists on dancing.

The Story as Told by Fonzie

"I practice all week until I limp home and I gotta soak my feet!"
"I spend 18 dollars and 50 cents on a monkey suit!"
"Two nerds come to my room, lock me in my bedroom and start calling me names!"
"Sherlock Holmes [Howard] here chases me and starts yelling at me!"
"Cunningham over there starts threatening me with physical violence!"
"Shortcake hits me in the leg!"
"And you want to go home happy? Well, let me tell you something, you're not going anywhere lady! The Fonz wants to dance!"

Here Fonzie discovers that Howard does have his allies. His love for Marion will have to continue being a guarded one. On the other hand, some aspects of their romance are more public.

> "Oh, Howard! It doesn't mean anything! Everybody
> kisses everybody in show business!"
>
> *—Marion*

How about those kisses? Marion showers them on Fonzie, and vice versa. Here is the eleven-year tally:

Fonzie from Mrs. C.: 79
Mrs. C. from Fonzie: 72
Others from either: 19

Howard seems completely oblivious. For instance, Marion decides to take part in a local production of "The Rainmaker" and Howard doesn't even notice that her co-star, Sloan Marlowe, is hitting on her. Fonzie does and chases Marlowe out of town. Fonzie then takes his place in the play, portraying Marion's love interest. Howard sits stupidly in the audience, applauding while another man holds his wife.

> "But there's nothing wrong with your shape, Mrs. C.!"
>
> *—Arthur Fonzarelli*

Indeed. How about those opening titles? In later seasons, Fonzie receives a kiss from Marion at the beginning of every show. In the next segment, Marion takes cake away from Howard before he's finished. This is sexual symbolism at its best. Is it any surprise then that Fonzie comes first in the credits, Marion second, and Howard . . . eighth?

During one episode Fonzie gets in bed right between Howard and Marion:

Marion: Arthur, maybe you didn't notice we're in bed.
Fonzie: Oh yeah, sure. I'm gonna be in and out just like the sandman.
Howard: Why don't you just slide up here between us?
Fonzie: Oh, come on, Mr. C. . . . not a bad idea!

Like Marion, "The Happy Days Reunion Special" takes the cake. Fonzie and Marion get a segment to themselves to discuss their particular relationship:

Fonzie: We had a lot of fun Marion . . . together.
Marion: We really did, Arthur.
Fonzie: You were the only one for eleven years that called me Arthur.
Marion: You were my Arthur. You'd put your head on my shoulder . . . I think you had a secret crush.
Fonzie: I did! I did!

Still not convinced? How about the necking scene between Fonzie and Marion from "the lost episode" (actually an outtake) shown during the Reunion Special? Fonzie and Marion kiss each other passionately while the rest of the Cunningham family go about their business as if nothing unusual was going on!

> "Oh Fonz, come on! Lay off the little old ladies, leave something for me!"
>
> —*Alfredo Delveccio*

Wait! That's not all! The Reunion Special also features another interesting outtake: Marion comes down from Fonzie's place, straightening her blouse, making sure her buttons are done up and fixing her hair. She glances around before blowing a kiss.

Fonzie and Other Married Women

Marion isn't the only married woman that Fonzie is messing around with. In the tennis club episode, Fonzie falls in love with an older married woman who has one of those "understandings" with her husband. Here's some startling dialogue:

Marion: Oh, you're going to do just fine. I bet you'll win the set six love.
Fonzie: Love?
Marion: Oh, that's right! I forgot to teach you about love!
Fonzie: Whoa! Mrs. C.!

Now, what's the story with Howard and Potsie?

Deviant Bowler Signals

The secret hand signals were put to paper, says Deviant Bowlers of America founder Julian Davis, to recruit new members and "keep people laughing when they are bowling badly." Besides **THE SECRET HANDSIGNALS OF THE DBA**, Julian also publishes Office Supply Junkie, Baby Split Bowling News, and International Swag. While the signals shown here are technically no longer a secret, a newer, more secret edition is under development.

Oily lanes

Eat this, you mook!

My beer has gone flat

Who took my wrist brace?

I thought you were payin'

Stop, in the name of love

Converted a baby split

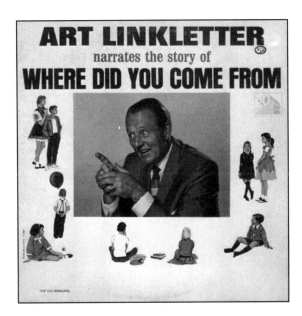

ART LINKLETTER
narrates the story of
WHERE DID YOU COME FROM

ѕє᙮ єↁ

Sex Ed on Vinyl

Like many zine publishers, Lynn Peril of **MYSTERY DATE** *is hooked on the discarded paperbacks that populate the far corners of thrift stores. She's particularly enamored with dating guides, beauty tomes, and marriage manuals—especially since she just got hitched—but she's never been known to pass up a good (or bad) sex education LP.*

Telling children about the facts of life has always caused a fine film of sweat to break out on parental upper lips. For squeamish adults, sex education records filled a void. What could be more folksy than entrusting your child to, say, Art Linkletter? Pick up a copy of "Art Linkletter Narrates the Story of Where Did You Come From" at your favorite thrift store and you'll see why. He explains all about frogs, chickens, horses, and humans and "what we call . . . the act of mating." Learn how the egg grows in "a hollow place in the mother's body that the doctor calls the uterus" and how the sperm gets to the egg through "a little tube" on the father's body. I guess Art doesn't know what the doctor calls it, or maybe he's not saying. Also, while he explains where to find "the little tube" on a horse, he never mentions where it might be located on a human male.

For answers to tricky questions like these, spin John and Joan McArdle's "Your Sexuality—A Thing of Beauty." Mr. McArdle, according to the liner notes, "was active in the Buffalo Family Life Department," while his wife "taught the High School Marriage Course in the Diocese of Buffalo." This is a fabulous record. For a couple who apparently went around making presentations to schools and parents' groups, you'd think they would have something more than a wooden stage presence. You can even hear them turning the pages of their notes. The McArdles are from the "now that you know all about it, don't do it" school, so they do name body parts and processes. But otherwise, the misinformation runs rampant. Joan explains that girls are "incapable" of having sex without "thinking of love." John tells them that they are fertile only one day a month. Oops! In fact, between that tidbit and a hot little surf number that closes side two, this record was probably responsible for untold numbers of teen pregnancies.

Teens probably couldn't believe that what they did in the backseats of cars and what John and Joan McArdle did in the marital bed were the same thing. "Don Lonie Talks to Teenagers," on the other hand, is a live recording before a high school assembly and Mr. Lonie has 'em rolling in the aisles. While technically not a sex education record, this album and a sequel, "Don Lonie Talks Again," are the aural equivalent of the "morality" unit of Family Living class. Lots of info about the dangers of drinking and driving (including a couple of teen auto dismemberment stories), wearing too much makeup, and conformity (at the expense of religion, of course)—all delivered in a wise-ass, deadpan manner. The moral here is go to church, please your parents, and grow up straight. And remember, "you can laugh at Don Lonie—but you can't laugh at God."

If you never had Don Lonie come to your high school to teach you how to be a squeaky clean adult, you might find yourself reaching for "The Way to Become The Sensuous Woman." (I know I did.) The liner notes stress "the importance of *his* orgasm" (their emphasis), so it's no surprise that what we have here is forty minutes of fashionable advice on how to give head. Which mental image do you prefer: the miniature vacuum cleaner, or the bunny nibbling asparagus? By the way, at an orgy, it's only polite to have sex with your escort first.

On the opposite end of the sexual spectrum sits Vonda Kay Van Dyke, Miss America 1965. Long before Bert Parks plunked that rhinestone tiara down on her head, Vonda Kay appeared in a film called *Teenage Diary*. After she became Miss America, Word Records ("The Christian Voice of the Audio Age") rushed an album into production containing excerpts from the film's soundtrack.

Teenage Diary is the story of drippy Penny Harris and her even drippier boyfriend, Brad Martin. It opens on prom night, as Penny (played by Vonda Kay, sounding like she's swallowed a dozen Quaaludes) gets ready for her date. Downstairs her creepy parents argue over the cost ($49.50) and scantiness of Penny's dress. Brad arrives, and Penny's parents give him the once over, insinuating that he and Penny will soon be rutting like crazed weasels.

If they only knew what Brad really had in mind. No sooner are they in the car than he's spouting scripture, and Penny is coyly asking if God told Brad to take her to the dance. As a matter of fact, he did. And so the three of them, Brad, Penny, and God, head off to "The Tiki Hut." Meanwhile, back at the homestead, Dad is bombed and makes a move on mom. Mom, who doesn't find a drunken rendition of "Danny Boy" to be adequate foreplay, declines.

Rejected, hubby decides to prove his manhood by searching for his whoring daughter. He finds her at the beach, where she and Brad, naked from the ankles down, are locked in their first embrace. Dad goes berserk, and beats the you-know-what out of Brad before dragging Penny home.

The next morning Penny goes to the hospital to visit Brad, who is just a wee bit reluctant to see her. Crying, she leaves his room to be cornered by his mom, who lectures her on the difference between real love (platonic and godly) and "self-gratification" (writhing teenage sex). Stupefied, Penny runs out of the hospital and into her old boyfriend, who just happens to be hanging around near his "sleek black Thunderbird." She hops in and they take off for "south of the border," where Penny gets loaded on tequila. She comes home drunk, tells her parents off, and steals the family car. Her parents enlist Brad (who has come over to apologize to Mr. Harris) to help look for her. They find her at Diamond Point, where she has just accepted Jesus into her life, and they all live happily ever after. The end.

The moral? Sex is evil, except for Christians, for whom it's boring and therefore all right.

Finally, for morals that make Vonda Kay look like an alley cat, consider one of the strangest records I own, "The Child Seducers." Essentially a tirade against the Sex Information and Education Counsel of the United States, this record from the World Christian Movement demonstrates how sex education is actually a communist plot. Narrated by John Carradine, the album begins with a rant about the torrent of filth overtaking this country. This includes the Smothers Brothers, who "skirt the thin line between pornography, good taste, and outright subversion," an "Oklahoma City Catholic church" that put up "nude statues for stations of the cross" and staged "dances for sex perverts," and sex education in the schools, which is nothing more than an evil plan to sow "the germinal seeds for America's final downfall" by creating an "entire generation of perverts and degenerates." Carradine goes on and on and on with unsubstantiated reports of kindergarten orgies and grade school bacchanals. Where was I? All I remember is a lousy Disney film about "your special day."

 Fond(led) Memories

When Skip Elsheimer developed a case of "burning writer's itch," he and Todd Morman remedied the situation with **PREPARATION X**. *In a moment of inspiration, they decided that their zine would "go after the inflamed opinions of swollen media wherever it finds them, inserting its suppositories of cynicism where they can do some good and smoothing on the ointment of enthusiasm as needed." Besides its great parody ads and media criticism ("Top Ten Media Sources That Should Shut the Hell Up"), Preparation X includes unexpected features such as collected anecdotes about childhood sexuality, from which this excerpt was taken. Todd wrote the introduction; the recollections were solicited from friends and readers.*

illustration by Michael Pilmer

When I was nine years old, my best friend Michael and I had a lot of fun playing spies. We'd chase each other around the neighborhood and then into his bedroom, where we'd take turns capturing each other. Then we'd pretend to tie each other up, and torture each other by tickling until the spy gave up the secret information. Fun, huh?

Well, um, it's actually more complicated than that. See, I remember being excited by all this. I mean, *really* excited. There was this funny feeling in my stomach, and both of us understood we were doing something that was different and a little naughty. One thing is clear: what my nine-year-old body was feeling as Michael and I rolled around on his bed can only be described as "horniness."

Does that shock you? God, I hope not. It's strange how we've ended up in a climate where even discussing the reality of pre-adolescent sexual arousal feels transgressive. Since few adults are willing to admit nine-year-olds can have sexual feelings, what kids end up with is a kind of DIY course in sexual education, fumbling around before our parents got home from work, sharing misinformation at slumber parties, and peeking in the closets and magazine stands of the adult world, hoping to find something resembling the truth.

Most of us got nothing more than a combination of awkward conversation, embarrassed silence, large doses of guilt ("Ohmigod! What are you two doing in there!"), and, if you were lucky, a copy of "Where Did I Come From?" Is it any wonder we turned to each other?:

• Around the second grade, I discovered that climbing a pole in gym class was stimulating. I then found that I could get just as stimulated by rubbing myself on a stuffed bear. I eventually rubbed the fur off one side of that bear. In the fourth grade, after looking at a friend's mother's *Playgirl*, I realized that certain vegetables looked like a penis. I would take cucumbers, carrots, and zucchinis from the refrigerator and . . . well, you can figure it out. Then I would get afraid that my mother would notice the missing vegetables, so I put them back in the fridge. I didn't think it was gross because I didn't eat salad.

• Once when I was sick my stepmom moved me into my sister's room so I wouldn't infect my brother (my sister was out of town). It was strange to read her books and play with her frilly stuffed animals. I felt like an invader behind enemy lines, but it was also great because I was alone and could let myself be like a girl and no one would call me names.

• I used to stay up by myself to watch "Saturday Night Live"—this was about age ten or eleven—and that's when I started touching myself. I didn't understand what I was doing or why, but I knew it was bad, because I'd go under the blanket and hide. When I first read about masturbation, I was like, "Wow, I was doing that years ago!"

• I remember vividly using my nightly good-night kiss on the lips from my mom as a way to find out what "real" kissing felt like. I tried to extend our kiss one night and she pulled back in horror. Oops. The night she caught me scratching my vagina (she apparently thought I was masturbating), she gave me a little speech which was obviously prepared in advance about how that was okay but this was not the time (I was supposed to be getting in the bath). I knew that if I

protested that I was not doing what she thought I was doing she would never believe me.

• My sister and I were bored sitting in the back seat on a long trip. I was eight and she was six. We thought it would be funny and gross to touch tongues, so we did. Mom asked what we were giggling about, so we told her. Mom and Dad missed the humor altogether, and made us promise never to do that again.

• When I was in the sixth grade a child molester got my phone number. He claimed to be my mother's gynecologist and asked me all kinds of personal questions on the phone about hair "down there," etc. He tried to tell me how to masturbate on the phone but I had no idea what he was talking about and did it wrong. He eventually convinced me to meet him in a school parking lot near my house where I showed myself to him, although he never touched me. After that I wouldn't talk to him on the phone anymore. I never told my mom.

• I remember, at age nine, sitting in the tub bathing while my mother was in the bathroom. She noticed my pubic hair. She asked me, "How long have you had that?" I said, "I always have," since I hadn't noticed any change. She said, "No, you haven't."

• I was at the beach, in the water with my cousin, and he convinced me to let him pee in my mouth. I was seven, he was eight. Both sets of parents saw us and got very upset. He got in trouble, but I just got the "some parts of our bodies we don't play with in public" talk.

• The first sexual feelings I remember occurred during a game called "See See Butt," which I invented with my cousins. At six, I was the oldest participant—the others were a female cousin, age five, two male cousins, ages one and three, and my two-year-old brother. The participants took turns going into a closet. The person in the closet closed the door, pulled down his or her pants, opened the closet door, and turned slowly for the viewing pleasure of the group. This game ended when one of the parents discovered us and we got spankings.

• When I was twelve there was this boy—he probably had a crush on me, now that I think back—who used to give me little gifts. We played this game in my bedroom where I would put a Starburst in my underwear and pretend to be asleep. He'd have to get it out without "waking" me.

• During fifth grade my friend Susan and I found a copy of *Penthouse* in the woods. That night we gawked at the women and decided to see if we looked the same "down there." We got a flashlight and were closely checking out each other's vaginas when Sue's mom walked in. Oh my God! She took away the magazine and the flashlight and then called my mom and told her I was corrupting her daughter. I wasn't allowed to sleep over at Sue's after that.

• There were tons of times in the swimming pool where some kid would spread his legs and you'd swim through them. When you got halfway through, the guy would close his legs, capturing you between them, and make you feel his balls or something. The pool was very heavily a kid-sex place to be.

• When I was eight I had a crush on Gail, this girl in my neighborhood. She was eight too, and the first girlfriend I ever had. I remember going into her bedroom one day, and how just being there felt naughty. I don't know whose idea it was, but we thought it would be fun to switch shoes, so she put on my "guy" shoes (probably Hush Puppies) and I put on her "girl" shoes while we were sitting on her bed. We knew it was wrong, so we were giggling and blushing. I remember this new feeling that I had, kind of weird but tingly and pleasurable. That was the first time I ever felt "sexual." The scary thing was that Gail's younger sister barged in on us; we quickly hid our feet under the bed. I remember the look on her face—she knew something strange was going on but couldn't figure it out. Getting caught like that made the whole thing even more exciting. I guess it's funny that I don't have this big shoe fetish.

slack

Slouching on the Shoulders of Giants

In this selection from the ninth issue of **STAY FREE!***, Jason Torchinsky finds the point where slacking and greatness meet.*

Perhaps the greatest injustice of modern society is that nobody comes around in a big truck every Thursday and hands us a fat check just for being ourselves. When I bring this up to politicians, they spout some sort of compulsively pragmatic rubbish like "That's impossible," or "There simply isn't enough money."

So we youths often acquiesce to performing menial tasks in exchange for currency. We're usually fairly certain that a properly trained chimpanzee could perform the job as well or better than we can, although we usually smell better.

These slacker jobs with lousy pay may not be particularly challenging, but they have one great advantage—they may not be particularly challenging. That means plenty of free time. I had this summer job with a pharmaceuticals company which was so lame I read *Moby Dick*, *Walden Two*, some book about those

Albert Einstein

German twins who made up their own language, *Heart of Darkness*, and spent an hour on the phone every morning with my friends who abused the company's 800 number.

Should I feel guilty? Should I lament that I did not utilize my work time for company projects? Absolutely not. I should feel proud to have landed a job that left me to my own pursuits, because I am in very good company. Some of the greatest thinkers of our age have done their best work while slacking.

Albert Einstein

A name now synonymous with frighteningly powerful intellect, Einstein held a job in the Swiss Patent Office for seven years. He began the job of technical officer in 1902 on a provisional basis; it wasn't until 1904 that he was hired. Although his salary was raised, he was not promoted because he was "not fully accustomed to matters of mechanical engineering." Einstein's responsibilities consisted of evaluating patent applications for fairly mundane devices such as cameras and typewriters. The job's starting pay, 3,500 Swiss francs, was lousy enough that he had to become a private physics tutor on the side.

More importantly, the job was undemanding, and young Albert knew how to stick it to the man, writing at least five papers on Brownian motion (the study of the motion of particles in liquids), mostly on work time. While these early writings were not connected with relativity, they laid the foundations for later works by utilizing single theories and laws for disparate phenomena and for the acceptance of a reality separate from what is observed.

Albrecht von Haller

Haller, a botanist, physician, and poet, is credited with writing the first standard physiology text between 1757 and 1766, as well as doing groundbreaking research on muscle contractility and writing poems about mountains. He did much of this work while employed as secretary of the Berne City Council. Records show that he was once reprimanded for writing a scientific treatise while a meeting was in session—but he was able to save his ass by reading back the detailed minutes that he had been keeping simultaneously.

Karl Marx

Karl Marx, the originator of Communism, was one of the most influential men in history. He read a lot and had a lifestyle remarkably similar to the perpetual grad students you see today—reading, jotting down notes for his earthshaking works, and annoying friends over coffee with complaints about How Things Suck and How He Would Do Things, and probably How Come I Can't Get a Date?

Karl got away with this because he had an analogue to the duped parents of today's grad-schoolers: Friedrich Engels. Engels was a wealthy owner of some English textile mills, and while lauded in our times as a great socialist thinker, he never utilized any of his progressive ideas of workers' reform in his factories, and Marx never pushed him to. Why? Because Karl needed his juice money. In fact, most of the correspondence between these two socialist giants can be boiled down to Marx's requests for more cash.

Charles Darwin

"Charles Darwin as a youth appears to have been a complete waster," writes biographer L. R. Croft. Charles' own dad told his son that "you care for nothing but shooting, dogs, and rat-catching and you will be a disgrace to yourself and your family."

With this type of encouragement, it's no wonder Darwin's first real job was lame. Not needing money because of his wealthy father, Charles accepted his now-famous position on the man o' war H.M.S. *Beagle.* He was not primarily the ship's naturalist, as is commonly believed, but rather a gentleman's companion to the aristocratic captain, Robert FitzRoy. FitzRoy desired someone of his own station to be his friend for the long voyage, and as a well-bred young graduate, Charles seemed to fit the bill.

Charles, however, did not get along with his boss, a pompous racist who hesitated to hire Darwin because of the shape of his nose. They quarreled often, and it was FitzRoy's hatred of Darwin that allowed the young man the extended shore treks through the Galapagos Islands and South America. FitzRoy was happy to have Darwin out of his sight for a while, and Darwin took advantage by compiling the voluminous notes on local species that eventually led to his theory of evolution and natural selection. Guess he showed them.

spirits

Lou Costello Speaks

The Reverend Speakers Gerald and Linda Polley, who founded **VOICES OF SPIRIT MAGAZINE** *in 1978 to "spread the teachings of those who have gone on before," are spiritists. Much of their zine is a discussion of their beliefs, but each issue also contains an interview with the spirit of a notable dead person such as Adolf Hitler ("Nazi 1"), Babe Ruth, or poet*

Phillis Wheatley. The couple interviewed Lou Costello, who died in 1959, in 1991.

Q: How did you and Abbott get back together in the Spirit World?

A: Well, he didn't like the guy who was standing in for him in the movies I was making. So he called up one day and said, "Lou, this guy's good, but he just isn't me! Let's put the old team back together!" And I said, "A-A-A-Abbott!"

Q: Are your films in the Spirit World done in the style of old Abbott and Costello movies?

A: It would be too difficult to list all the productions that we have done in Spirit. But I will give you a couple of examples. Last year we did "Abbott & Costello Meet Han Solo." In this adventure we played two screwy alien professors who hold a secret that will save the Alliance from Imperial destruction. And Han Solo must get them from Tatooine to the secret rebel base. He accomplishes the task, but not without a great deal of difficulty, most of it caused by the bumbling nature of his passengers. The second production we did that year was "Abbott & Costello Meet the Spaced Invaders." As the invaders leave Earth, they stumble across the remains of a rocket launched by a mad scientist twenty years before. They revive its two occupants and take them back to Mars. Mars is never the same again! Our style is our trademark. If we change that, there'd be no sense in us making movies at all. I guess we still do a good job because we pack 'em in!

Q: If you could do a movie now, what would it be about, and who would co-star?

A: An incredible question! I would like to do a comedy portraying Mikhail Gorbachev with Abbott as Boris Yeltsin, and we'd call it "Which Way Went the Party?" or "Not That Way, Comrade!" with Madonna as my wife.

ZINE VOICES

"I like pondering on just how someone in The Netherlands or Australia heard about my zine. It's like a wonderfully demented virus."

—Ralph Coon, *The Last Prom*

Milkcrate Sports

*Architecture student John Freeborn strives to "find new ways to see the beauty and style in milkcrates that few recognize." **MILKCRATE DIGEST** is stacked with photos of milkcrates ("Theft of This Case is a Crime"), ideas for building with milkcrates, and utilitarian uses for milkcrates (cereal bowl, checkers table, chair, bar, fencing helmet, condom). The first issue also includes a pop-up crate like those crazy kids' books might have, and issue 2 comes with* Milkcrate Sports Illustrated, *in which these photographs appeared.*

Can't Beat Sisyphus

After rewriting Huck Finn with a modern twist (page 72), Steve Steinberg of **MEANWHILE . . .** *gave a similar treatment to another legendary outdoorsman.*

Illustration by Vance Lehmkuhl

"Welcome back. We're about halfway up the mountain right now, and the man they all came to see is not disappointing. After his usual slow start, he's really picked things up, and as we get back to the action, the standing-room-only crowd is really getting behind him. Let there be no mistake . . . Sisyphus knows how to work an audience!

"There! . . . the fake slip. If I've seen it once, I've seen it a thousand times, and I always fall for it. My friends, I'm sorry that radio just can't do it justice. Oh, the way he drops to his right knee—the ankle, looking for all the world like it just got crushed under the weight of his enormous rock . . . it really is a hoot! He mugs a smile at some fans in the front row. How he manages to hold up that stone while pretending to be hurt is beyond me. The power that man must have!

"And speaking of power, wait'll you see the new Sisyphus calendar. It'll be out in time for the holidays. I just got ahold of an advance copy and, my golly, you should see some of these pictures. Wow! We should all be in that kind of shape at his age. This would make a great gift for anybody. I don't know if I'd give one to my wife or girlfriend, though—she'll never take her eyes off it!

"No sooner do I mention wives and girlfriends and Sisyphus has gone into his . . . oh, how would I put this . . . his popular derriere wiggle. I don't know where he came up with it. It has become something of a trademark with him. To tell you the truth, I don't see what all the fuss is about, but I guess what I think doesn't matter to the throngs of women that whoop and whistle like rabid construction workers whenever he does that little dance.

"You know, you can build up a mighty big thirst just listening to Sisyphus push that rock up the hill, so why not quench that thirst with an icy cold Budweiser? Nothing beats The King Of Beers—Budweiser.

"As we reach the three-quarters mark, let's take a break before the homestretch and dip into the mailbag and pull out another couple of winners in the "Why I Want to Be Like Sisyphus" contest. Winners will receive two cases of any Coke product and be eligible to win a trip for four to Disneyland for the opening of the new "Sisyphus's Mountain" rollercoaster. Our first lucky winner is Jennifer Di . . . Pasquale—Jennifer DiPasquale. Jennifer is eight and writes, "I would like to be like Sisyphus because he's very strong. I would like to able to push his rock. It looks fun. The end." That was sweet, Jennifer. Next, we hear from Stewart Becker . . . and Stewart is fourteen. He writes, "I want to be like Sisyphus, because he is a good role model for kids like me. He took a bad situation like being punished by the gods, and turned it into a good situation. I would also like to be like him because he is rich and very influential." Well, thank you, Stewart. Both Jennifer and Stewart will have their names entered into our big jackpot drawing. Good luck to both of you.

"We're just about in sight of the mountain top. The weather has been excellent. There had been some talk of showers, but thankfully they have held off. He's really cranking now. This is pure power. This is really—Wait! What the heck is he doing? I can't believe what I just saw. He gave the rock a mighty push, then turned around and started . . . miming, like Charlie Chaplin. He pretended he didn't know the rock was about to roll back into him! At the last second, he turned and caught the thing, but, my golly, was that a funny bit. And so unexpected. This is usually the part of the mountain where he really has his game face on. Oh boy, the crowd sure enjoyed that. I'll be darned . . .

"Sisyphus might know what fate holds for him, but unfortunately the same can't be said for you or me. That's why we need The Kemper Group. Trust The Kemper Group for all your insurance needs.

"And it looks like he's about to do it again! He's reached the mountain top. What an iron man. What a model of consistency and longevity. He's incredible. He takes off his wrap-around Oakley sunglasses, wipes the perspiration from his brow, and shakes a victorious fist at the fans gathered at the peak. They love him! And there goes the rock! It rolls past him on its way down. He blows it a kiss, and asks for some applause for his silent co-star. What a show this guy puts on. Now he's heading back down the mountain. He'll shake hands and give high-fives all the way down. And we'll be back with the Tower Records "Roll That Rock Recap" . . . right after this."

Penalty Boxes:
The World of Hockey Fight Videos

Growing up in Boston, Don Steinberg was a huge Bruins fan. He wasn't much of a fighter, though. "I was in one fistfight as a kid, and I've been preparing for another one ever since," says Don, editor of **MEANWHILE . . .** *He gets his tips from the pros.*

A few winters ago, I met Lyndon Byers, then a brash young forward for the Boston Bruins. Byers was never known to avoid a good fight on the ice, and when someone asked him to expound on the topic, every guy in the room turned silently to listen.

What, we all wanted to know, is the sequence of events that turns ordinary hockey into a violent brawl? And what, for Pierre's sake, are the players yammering at each other before they go at it?

To the best of my recollection, Byers' answer went as follows: First, a player gets slammed against the boards. To the guy who did it, he yells, "Fuck you." Then the guy who did it replies, "Fuck you." The victimized player then retorts, "Yeah? Well, fuck you." Upon which the guy who delivered the slam answers conclusively, "Fuck you." Finally, one player takes a swing, and the conversation is over.

That's how it's done by professionals. Any connoisseur of the sport has a certain body of knowledge about this facet of the game. But understanding hockey fights serves a greater purpose. By their nature, hockey fights are completely unnecessary and useless. They are cubes of testosterone thawing out before your eyes. To understand how these confrontations develop is to face the caged animal within us all.

Fortunately, there is an entire underworld of activity devoted to understanding human nature. There are people on this continent who painstakingly assemble videotapes of hockey fights, one violent battle after another, carefully editing out parts of hockey games that do not contain fights. Many of these tape-makers trade with each other; others sell them.

After spotting a small ad in the back of *Hockey Digest*, I ordered the "Fists of Fury" catalogue, which describes forty such compilations. Each video's fights are listed as if they were tracks on a record album. For example, a particular 45-second segment might be titled "K. Muller Suckers Gordie Roberts" or "T. O'Reilly Pulls Brian Hextall Jr.'s Hair" or simply "L. Byers vs. G. Odjuck." There are even 90-minute tapes dedicated to individual players known for their brawling techniques. The tape that caught my fancy was a team feature: "Vintage Bruins Fights, 1969–80."

When my tape arrived, I was thrilled to learn that the Bruins fights it illegally reproduced were from the original TV broadcasts. This meant they'd be described by announcers Fred Cusick and Johnny Pearson. Cusick and Pearson loved the Bruins and, like any hockey announcers, considered fighting skills to be a standard part of a complete player's tools. They were audibly excited whenever a fight would erupt. Here, for example, is the verbatim call by Cusick of a scrap between Bruin Wayne Cashman and Blackhawk Keith Magnuson: "Bobby Hull shoots wide . . . Ravlich trying to move it out . . . deflects [sound of whistle] and here's Magnuson and Cashman going now! Look at that left! Look at that left from Cashman! Cashman down! Look at Magnuson! Oh, what a fight! Cashman tremendous here! Oooohhh, that's one of the best fights you'll see anywhere!"

The fight lasted about six seconds. Pearson could become even more agitated. He would also call a fight everything but a fight: it was a "real wingding," a "brouhaha," a "donnybrook." When, in one early seventies video clip, a round of preliminary groping by annoyed players failed to advance into a brawl, Pearson sounded disappointed. "That looks like a real love-in down there now."

One scene that somehow made it onto "Vintage Bruins" twice shows Terry O'Reilly sitting on the chest of aging hockey legend Frank Mahavolich, whose legs flail like a bug while O'Reilly incessantly pounds him in the head. As the Boston Garden crowd roars with pleasure, Pearson's nasal Canadian brogue sums up: "There's no doubt about who's the most popular player on the Bruins at this moment!"

"And the fans love it," says Cusick a few moments later, as Al Simmons absorbs some facial blows from Canadian J. C. Tremblay. Fans caught on camera have their faces pressed against the Plexiglas safety wall. They're screaming, cheering, pounding each other on the back. They can't believe they're seeing this. Guys fighting!

These, remember, were the days before the Third Man In penalty, which now requires ejection of any player who joins a fight already in progress. Back then, you had goalies jumping onto huge piles of skaters, or entire teams ganging up on one man. One prolonged scene on the tape shows Buffalo Sabre Jim Schoenfeld exchanging blows with Cashman in the runway where the Zamboni is stored, while Terry O'Reilly and Jim Lorenz lead a donnybrook on the Buffalo bench. "Fred," exclaims Pearson as the action finally wears down, "there's only one word for this, and that's gotta be . . . ridiculous."

FREE ADVICE

"The founder of *Factsheet Five*, Mike Gunderloy, once told that the typical half-life of a zine is one year. Try to beat that."

—Jim Hogshire, *Pills-a-Go-Go*

stalkers

Looking for Mr. Isaak

Daniel Drennan is a curious guy, and that curiosity is reflected in **INQUISITOR**. *In one issue he described how to build a graphical user interface with parts from Radio Shack; others have included observations about life in New York, a fond look at toys like the Fisher Price PXL 2000 video cam, and Marlene Taylor's sidebar (below) to a longer piece examining modern surveillance. "It's about the traces we leave," says Daniel, "and what others do with them." Adds Marlene, "Chris, if you're reading this, I'm not stalking you. Honest."*

Why do we do these things? Look, I'm not psychotic, really. I just got a little too involved with the guy, and I'm over it now. The guy in question is Chris Isaak—he of the broad shoulders and "Wicked Game" (or "The Yodeling Song"), and a few summers ago I became rather too interested in him. I wanted to find out more about him, his life, his history, what he was before he was a semi-famous pop star. And you know what? It was easy.

First I went to the library and made copies of all the articles I could find about him, starting with the earliest interviews. Wannabes often share lots of interesting personal info which they would never dream of saying to interviewers once they have a hit in the Top 10. I found out that he was from Stockton, California; that he had stayed there until moving to San Francisco in the early eighties; that he went to the University of the Pacific; and that his family still lived in Stockton. Although he claims he now lives in San Francisco, I couldn't find any public records for him in the city (such as voter registration—if he's voting, he's not voting in San Francisco).

So I took a road trip to Stockton and went to the public library, the source of all data. Here I found his family listed in the 1990 phone book. I also found listings for him and his family in the city register going back before he was born. Most small towns have some kind of city register which may show not only names and addresses but ages and occupations of family members. The library at the University of the Pacific offered up a yearbook which contained not him, but his mother—and her maiden name.

Using that little gem, I was able to order a copy of his birth certificate from the county clerk's office (which I keep tucked away with my tax forms, thank you very much). I also determined which high school he attended, but the library didn't have his yearbook (they did have one for his brother, who had graduated a few years before).

Up to this point, I had done everything completely legal and above board. But since it was the library's fault that it was missing his yearbook, and since it was a public high school, I figured a tiny deception was okay. I went to the high school with a partner in crime and told them we needed to look at the yearbooks because we were doing some kind of sociology report on the Central Valley, blah blah blah, and they believed us. They let us take all the yearbooks into the faculty lounge and look at them to our heart's content. They even let us use their copy machine.

I probably could have gotten his tax records, too, but I didn't have his Social Security number and I didn't feel like spending the time on the phone to get it. The last thing I did was to drive past his parents' house, where his dad was washing the family car; I stopped and asked directions and he was very nice to me.

stunts

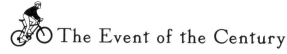 The Event of the Century

*Steve Mandich, who grew up imitating Evel Knievel on a banana seat bike (*right*), dedicates much of his zine,* **HEINOUS,** *to the King of Stuntmen. A notorious drinker and womanizer who once owed the IRS millions in back taxes, Evel retired from stunt work in 1980 to hone his artistic skills—the daredevil who once soared with the birds now paints them. Steve, meanwhile, had no inkling Heinous would rocket ahead when he completed the first issue on his twenty-fifth birthday. It all just came together: He worked at a copy shop, and he had time on his hands.*

The dream came to him in 1966 at Moose's Place Saloon in Kalispell, Montana. Loaded on Montana Marys, Evel Knievel eyed a calendar on the wall depicting the Grand Canyon. With his motorcycle jumping career well underway, he suddenly realized what would become the ultimate challenge of his life, the biggest death trip of all. Said Evel, "I ain't afraid of a damn thing."

Initially the titanic leap was conceived as an ultra-long jump on a specially-boosted cycle. With further analysis, it became clear that such a feat would be impossible on just a motorcycle; it would have to be a modified rocket shot if it were to work at all. Evel unsuccessfully appealed to the Department of the Interior for airspace over the National Park, so his sights shifted to a

OPEN UP AND BLEED

A FIELD GUIDE TO EVEL'S INJURIES

"Color Me Lucky" was Evel Knievel's motto and it couldn't have been more fitting; perhaps the most amazing aspect of his career was living to tell about the staggering extent of bodily harm he sustained. According to the *Guinness Book of World Records*, Evel broke an astounding 433 bones in the 15-year span of his daredevilry. It is a truly remarkable number that Evel likes to downplay, insisting he never broke more than 60. Doing some homework, that averages out to each of his 206 bones breaking slightly more than twice, timewise a break about every 12 days. Evel spent more than half the years 1966 to 1973 in a wheelchair or on crutches, and today he's essentially one twisted mass of scar tissue and fractures from head to toe. Along with the 10 steel plates and several metal pins set into him, he could bring even the mightiest health insurance company to their knees. Evel has proven to be built like a Mack Truck, and his mindless bravery in the name of America surely is deserving of an honorary purple heart. Here's a graphic sampling of Evel's damages, by no means whatsoever a comprehensive listing. Let's break it down:

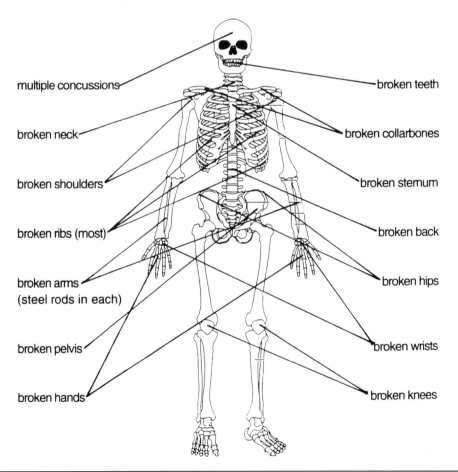

multiple concussions

broken neck

broken shoulders

broken ribs (most)

broken arms
(steel rods in each)

broken pelvis

broken hands

broken teeth

broken collarbones

broken sternum

broken back

broken hips

broken wrists

broken knees

spot where he once fished with his grandfather, the Snake River Canyon in Twin Falls, Idaho. The chasm is far narrower and shallower than the Grand, but either jump could be fatal nonetheless. Evel leased three hundred acres of land at the site and made further preparations.

To build the pseudo-rocketship he enlisted the engineering talents of Bob Truax, who Evel falsely claimed worked for NASA. The prototype X-1 SkyCycle was test fired in 1973, but it smashed into the canyon rocks below. A second test sent it plunging into the depths of the Snake's green waters. Going back to the drawing board, Truax came up with the X-2 SkyCycle, a steam-powered rocket made from a Navy bomber's fuel tank. The water for the steam came from Washington's Tumwater River, by no coincidence the same water that Evel's corporate sponsor Olympia Beer uses. The $1 million X-2 measured 13 feet long and weighed 1,300 pounds, built with exact specifications to clear the 3/4-mile distance across the 600-foot-deep canyon. The contraption was registered with the FAA as an unmanned aircraft, since Evel had little control over it. He would merely fire the ignition with his left hand and open the drag chutes with his right. In the event of an emergency, Evel would have to bail out with a parachute.

Some physics came into play: launching the X-2 off the 108-foot ramp pitched at 56 degrees required 5,000 pounds of thrust to reach a top speed of 400 miles per hour, sending it 2,000 feet above the canyon's rim. Evel would pull in five g's of force, but would wear no g suit. Parachutes would open at the zenith, and then the craft would gently float down to land on the opposite rim. The total projected shot was calculated at 4,781 feet.

During the preceding week, the carnivalesque hype kicked into high gear, covered by a media circus 130 strong. An estimated 200,000 spectators were projected to pay $25 to line the canyon's rim to witness the "Event of the Century," and millions more would spend $10 apiece to watch it live on closed-circuit television. Famous oddsmaker Jimmy the Greek figured "Evel would have a better chance playing Russian roulette. . . . It's three to one he's crazy." Top Rank boxing promoter Bob Arum paid Evel $6 million up front for a cut of the lucrative action, and Evel would eventually gross $9 million altogether. The two hustlers had an uneasy relationship; Evel was once heard to explode, "The greatest day of my life is being run by a bunch of goddamn Jews!" He spent the week playing golf with decrepit former boxing champ Joe Louis and tennis goofball Bobby Riggs, and held several rhetoric-laden press conferences. Butte's favorite son bragged about his supposed million-dollar pre-jump bash: "If you think Jesus had a Last Supper, wait until you see mine!" The "supper" was merely an egomaniacal Evel barhopping around town tossing out cans of beer.

Finally the day arrived, September 8, 1974. With temperatures approaching 90 degrees and winds turning the area into a dust bowl, a disappointing 15,000 people descended upon the site. Among the straights in the crowd were large contingents of Jesus freaks, drugged-up hippies, and beer-swilling outlaw motorcycle gangs. Many biker chicks went topless; one naked woman was hurled over a fence into the press compound. The hired security consisted of shotgun-toting rednecks and 150 cycle-gang types, reminiscent of the Rolling Stones' security force of Hell's Angels at Altamont. An ugly mob formed, burning down concession stands, looting beer and vandalizing a fire engine. If not for Evel's dubious security team, it would have torched the SkyCycle itself. A nervous Evel remarked, "I've created a monster, and I don't know how to control it."

A priest led the audience in prayer, Evel's poem "Why?" and "The Ballad of Evel Knievel" blared from loudspeakers, a high school marching band played the National Anthem, and then

Evel was hoisted into the X-2 on the Freedom Crane. The magnificently orchestrated drama would soon be over.

At 3:36 P.M. Evel blasted off, white steam sending dirt and gravel flying out over the crowd. Before the X-2 even cleared the ramp, a mechanical failure blew out the drogue chute prematurely. The force tore off Evel's escape parachute as the airborne X-2 spun helplessly out of control. Many spectators screamed, others prayed loudly, some wept. The bikers yelled "Fuck him in the ass!" The TV crews abandoned their equipment as the crowd crashed the fence and surged toward the canyon edge for a better view. The SkyCycle's drogue chute untangled itself and pulled out the main chute, slowing the falling rocket. A northwest wind forced it to drift back towards the canyon's near wall, twisting downward into the abyss. The X-2 landed on some rocks by the river, where rescue boats freed Evel from the craft and helped him into a helicopter. One of the rescuers was left behind, forced to spend the cold night down in the canyon. He wrapped himself in the X-2's parachutes for warmth and climbed out the next day.

> ## ZINE VOICES
>
> "Why publish? Why has nothing to do with it—it's an imperative. Why do people who like gardening grow things? Why do people who like woodworking build things? Why do mountain climbers climb things?"
> —Paul Lukas, *Beer Frame*

Back on the rim, the unruly mob trashed and torched about all that was left at the site: fences, telephone and utility poles, television equipment, and toilets. By day's end the launch ramp itself went up in flames. Earlier in the day, President Gerald Ford officially pardoned Richard Nixon for his Watergate shenanigans. Evel was understandably pissed that it would be the headlines on all the papers the next morning instead of him. The following Saturday the event aired on "ABC's Wide World of Sports," a spectacle which *Sports Illustrated* would pronounce "A noble failure, far more exciting than a letter-perfect leap could ever have been." Evel was now a bigger star than ever.

Today on the canyon's edge stands a six-foot-high granite commemorative memorial with the X-2 SkyCycle etched into it. The inscription reads, "From this point on September 8th, 1974, Evel Knievel attempted a mile-long leap of the Snake River Canyon." The rock of ages implores that we never forget.

> ## ZINE VOICES
>
> "A friend and I published one issue of a zine called *La Luna* (our plan was to publish according to the lunar calendar). He was in a save-the-world phase and I was out to make fun of it. The result was a zine with a serious case of split personality. The first issue had an interview with the head of a hunger relief organization (his story) and a piece on having diarrhea on a first date (mine)."
> —Benjamin Serrato, *15 Minutes*

The Shaneshaw Redemption

Writing for **HITCH**'s *eleventh issue, Brad Lott (brother of the editor, Rod) chronicles a day in the life of a grade school daredevil whose training wheels came off before he was born.*

His name is Shane Shaw. He stands 4'3" and weighs 160 pounds. He's ten years of age. A hefty young buck, but a lad with balls of steel. His passion: stunt riding.

It is not by design, however, that this youngster stumbled upon a thrill-seeking pastime of tricks and spills, but rather sheer dumb luck, too many hours of chips and Nintendo, and the apparent lack of a decent education. What follows is a day of terrors following this crafty stuntboy as he rides balls-out on his two-wheeled cycle of doom.

Shane: It's a nice day. Perfect for flips.
Hitch: You can do flips.
Shane: Sometimes.

He chuckles, his round face jiggling. Shane is outfitted in corduroy pants, a white tank-top, and fly Vans. His rolls of flab equip him with the padding he needs for this dangerous sport. I notice just how much alike he and his fourteen-year-old sister look in a tank-top. He carries his trademark three-liter Coca-Cola, which is almost empty, and it's only noon.

Hitch: Shane, let's start by going over some highlights from your past, some stories of triumph in the face of impending danger.
Shane: Huh?
Hitch: Tell me about some tricks you've pulled.
Shane: I can pop good wheelies.
Hitch: And?
Shane: I like to use cats as props in my stunts. I've done a lot of ramping. I almost jumped my parents' fence once. I can jump the shrubs over there, too.
Hitch: Let's see.

Shane takes off with the vigor of a true daredevil. He makes the jump with ease. He returns, breathless.

Hitch: So how many bike wrecks have you been in?
Shane: Oh, say, more than a hundred.
Hitch: What happened during your last big wreck?
Shane: I whammed my jaw into a metal fence at the church and the fence fell off.
Hitch: Did the crash damage your bike?
Shane: It was my mom's bike. The rim got bent and the pedal fell off.
Hitch: Tell me another one.

Shane: When I ramped off my big blue ramp, I landed on my head and my toe got broke. I peeled some skin off my knee and I got racked. I also lost a shoe and my mom gave me licks.

Hitch: Why is it you try and ramp things?

Shane: I want to be a stuntman when I grow up.

Hitch: Does your mother get mad when you wreck your bike?

Shane: No, she doctors up my head, legs, and stuff. One time I wrecked and said "Shit!" and she heard me, but I learned it from her.

Hitch: What tricks can we see you accomplish in the near future?

Shane: Well, me and my friend Justin put hairspray on my ramp and lit it, but the flames went out before I got to it. We're gonna try gasoline Saturday.

Hitch: Where did you get the idea?

Shane: I saw it at the fair.

Hitch: Where do you get the courage to perform such dangerous stunts?

Shane: Well, my mom says I'm always rowdy cuz I drink so much soda. She says I'm always climbin' the rafters.

Hitch: Do you ever solve crimes while riding your bicycle?

Shane: Sort of.

Hitch: Let's see some more tricks, Shane.

After some discussion of what exactly I want to witness, Shane demonstrates some tricks he swears he made up himself. He pulls what he calls his "Michael Jackson," his "Big Booty Hoe,"

The "MICHAEL JACKSON"

1. GAIN SPEED	2. POP UP	3. SWIVEL 180°	4. FALL & CRY

and his "Power Ranger."

I also see him knock down a pile of bricks and wheelie through the neighbor's garden. He "bunny-hops" over a potted plant, wrecks into a bush, and cries.

Even tough stunt guys lose it now and then. Shane regains his composure and limps toward me.

Hitch: Are you alright?

Shane: Yeah, that wasn't bad. I didn't break nothin'. One time I jumped a 50-foot tree and landed on my butt.

The "BIG BOOTY HOE"

1. GAIN SPEED	2. POP UP	3. JUST RIDE & RIDE	4. FALL & CRY

Hitch: Wow, 50 feet, huh?

Shane: Yeah, I think it was that tall. (He measures out somewhere around four feet.) I can also jump cars! Wanna see?

Hitch: Sure. Go for it.

Shane: Alright. Hang on.

He sets his blue ramp up next to his mom's green El Camino, but his mother catches him and puts a stop to his daring attempt.

"Blubbers!" she yells. "Get the hell off a there!" Shane retreats.

Hitch: Why does your mom call you Blubbers?

Shane (obviously tortured): Shut up, you!

After a short walk, we reach a playground which houses a huge metal swingset, two colossal slides, and a tire swing. Shane races through the parking lot and jumps a parking block so he can slide his bike along a fence rail. He falls, bounces, and, once again, cries.

This time, it takes some coaxing to get him to resume his trickin'.

Hitch: Are you injured?

Shane: Nah, I'm just bleeding a little. I've done that before. Man, my mom's gonna be mad.

Undaunted by his spill, Shane remounts his bike and speeds toward the slides.

Shane: I'm gonna flip off'a *that!*

Hitch: Alright. Be careful.

My confidence in him, though, is shaken. Shane rides toward the slide, giving himself plenty of headstart. He darts up the slide, clears the top and sails high in the air. He attempts a flip, but starts it far too late, a matter of two to three feet from the ground, which is speeding toward him.

The "POWER RANGER"
1. GAIN SPEED 2. POP UP 3. FLIP UP 4. FALL & CRY

Upon impact, many sick noises are audible. He twists, grinds, bounces, and spins along the dirt and rock, a cloud of dust sparing me from the grisly carnage. And then, he cries.

I run over to him, fearing a lawsuit.

Hitch: Are you alright, Shane?

Shane (between sniffles): I'm alright . . . I don't want to . . . do any more tricks . . . today.

As we head home, he stops crying. I realized he is finished for today, but will ride proud again tomorrow. He has the heart of a lion. I wonder if he will ever attempt the slide stunt again, or how next Saturday's fire trick will go.

Hitch: What will you call the famous slide jump trick, Shane?

Shane: (pausing courageously): I don't know.

"I don't know," I think to myself. Man, what a crafty trickster.

Frequently Asked Questions About Wheelies

Before sharing this definitive article from the third issue of **HEINOUS**, *Steve Mandich updated the wheelies records exclusively for* The Book of Zines.

Q: What is a "wheelie"?
A: The wheelie is the most basic and common of all bicycle stunts. It is performed by riding with the front wheel balanced in midair while the rear wheel remains on the ground. This may also be accomplished on a motorcycle.

Q: How long must the front wheel be in the air to be considered a wheelie?
A: There is no governing body regulating wheelies to establish any officially sanctioned wheelie rules, however, maintaining at least a temporary balance on the rear wheel would seem acceptable.

Q: Who coined the term "wheelie"?
A: Leonardo da Vinci.

Q: Who can do wheelies?
A: Practically anyone who can ride a road bike, mountain bike, BMX bike, cruiser, or lowrider.

Q: Can a car do a wheelie?
A: Yes, but the front two wheels must be airborne while the rear wheels stay on the ground. This is a very difficult maneuver to perform with a front-wheel-drive vehicle. Most any land-based, multi-wheeled vehicle can do a wheelie, so long as the front end can become airborne. This includes tricycles, skateboards, and wheelchairs. RVs, trains, and monorails cannot do wheelies.

Q: Can a unicycle do a wheelie?
A: Technically, no. True, balance is maintained on a single wheel, but by definition a wheelie can only be done with a multi-wheeled vehicle.

Q: Can a boat do a wheelie?
A: No, and neither can a helicopter nor an airplane, except for a few moments during takeoff.

Q: Can a blimp do a wheelie?
A: No.

Q: Aren't wheelies dangerous?
A: No. Injury can be avoided as long as common sense is exercised and the proper equipment is used. Alcohol may impede wheelie ability and result in loss of control.

Q: Has anyone ever been killed doing a wheelie?
A: No such incidents have been kept on record so a precise number, if any, would be difficult to gauge.

Q: Aren't wheelies illegal?
A: According to the Oregon State Motor Vehicle Code, wheelies and other vehicular stunts are prohibited on all public thoroughfares. Laws may vary by state.

Q: Is there any difference between "do a wheelie," "ride a wheelie," and "pop a wheelie"?
A: No, the terms are synonymous and can be used interchangeably. "Wheelie" may be used both as a noun ("The man does a wheelie") and as a verb ("The man wheelies").

Q: Is there anyone named after wheelies?
A: Yes, Ms. Bon Von Wheelie of Tacoma, Washington.

Q: How fast can a wheelie be ridden?
A: 157.87 miles per hour. Belgian Jacky Vranken set this world speed record for motorcycle wheelies at Belgium's St. Truiden Military Airfield on November 8, 1992.

Q: How long can a wheelie be ridden?
A: Four hours, 21 minutes, and 1 second. Robert Hurd set this wheelie duration record at the Recreation Centre in Winchester, England on November 18, 1986.

Q: How far can a wheelie be ridden?
A: Yasuyuki Kudoh popped a 205.7-mile wheelie without stopping or touching the front wheel to the ground in Tsukuba City, Japan, on May 5, 1991. American Doug Domokos previously held the record with a 145-mile wheelie at the Alabama Motor Speedway on June 27, 1984. "The Wheelie King" stopped only because he ran out of gas.

Q: How can I do a wheelie on my bicycle?
A: Pull hard upwards and rearwards on the handlebars while simultaneously pushing harder on the pedals, but not so hard that you fall completely over the back wheel. This works best on a flat, firm surface.

Q: Is there any secret to doing a wheelie?
A: Practice, practice, practice.

Market Research

Darin Johnson and his buddies Dagwood Reeves, Leif Hanson, and Nathan Curley realized one day that sharks are kinda cool. But how universal was this feeling? The only way to find out was a survey of total strangers. They briefly considered asking passersby about racecar drivers instead, but Dagwood offered this: "Pretend you're playing a game of rock-paper-scissors. Whichever symbol you choose is still vulnerable to defeat by another symbol. Well, the shark says, 'Fuck symbols' and eats your hands, leaving you to wonder why you were using your opposable thumbs to play a game instead of fashioning harpoons." The Society of Shark Fear was born, as was its handbook, **SHARK FEAR, SHARK AWARENESS**.

Hi, wanna shark flyer? It's chock full of interesting tidbits about shark history, trivia, behavior, and shark anecdotes.

Wanna hear a joke?

Why'd the shark cross the road?

To eat its young.

I made that up myself. If you tell that joke to anyone you have to give me royalties. But before you run off and tell it to your friends, why'ncha read this flyer? Y'know, sharks have been around for so long, 400 million years in fact—well, it's either 400 million or 400 billion, I can't remember—but they have been around since long before Jesus, and long before most modern plant-life, and even long before the first thumbs were first twiddled. It's true.

Y'know why sharks have been around that long? Y'know why sharks have stuck around through the thick and thin of evolution? Because they're perfect, that's why. They couldn't evolve any better if you stapled opposable thumbs to their flippers. They'd probably bite them off anyway. Jesus! Do you know what that means? Do you realize the implications of that? It means that this big ol' fuckin' ball of stench called Mother Nature has given birth to a creature that is the personification of Nature's ideal. And that ideal is relentless feeding with no excuses. The shark jets around silently in the murk eating whatever is big enough to fit in its mouth. Nature's a goddamn greedy two-year-old with big fuckin' choppers, that's what. But, unlike a two-year-old, it's not just a stage. That's the scary part. Nature has rewarded the shark's incessantly violent behavior with the Grade A stamp of 100 percent evolutionary success.

—Tiny brains? Tiny brains?

Now you're just trying to make yourself feel better. That brain of yours ain't big enough to keep that wonderfully complex personality of yours out of the shark's digestive system. Yeah, they got tiny brains, but that too is rewarded. If sharks were a little smarter they'd show some sense and not chow on every piece of skank that floats their way. Or maybe their brains could get even bigger and they might have a little spark of compassion for a wee little fishy, until one day the shark would carve a nice path of morality through the ocean's depths.

Y'know what I think about that? Y'know what I think about sharks with big brains? I think that if sharks had big brains we wouldn't be sittin' here talkin' about sharks. Y'know why we wouldn't be talkin' about sharks? Cuz there wouldn't be any fuckin' sharks. Let me tell you a little story: One day some fishermen caught a shark. They slit open its belly and all its guts fell back into the ocean. What would you do if your guts fell into the ocean? Yeah, I don't know either. But I sure as hell know what I wouldn't do. If I was shoved into the ocean, floatin' along there right next to my guts, I wouldn't start chowin' on my own guts. Jesus! The irony!

—You're not an environmentalist, are you? You don't sound like an environmentalist. It sounds to me like you wanna kill off these beasts. That's good. Here, wanna balloon? The balloon's symbolic of a pufferfish. Sharks stay away from pufferfish cuz they know what's what. The ancestors of today's modern shark used to try and eat pufferfish and . . . y'ever gag on a lollipop? Same story. Gotta lick 'em. Maybe if sharks had tongues they'd try and lick pufferfish, but I think they probably have better things to do.

Hey, what do sharks and environmentalists have in common? I made this up just now.

If their brains were any bigger they wouldn't be zealous enough and their species would die out in a pathetic fit of compromise.

Yeah, sorry. Guess I won't be gettin' many royalties from that one.

Sixty–Six Things I Hate about Shopping in Thrift Stores

If you've ever stumbled on an unused paint-by-numbers kit, a pristine copy of "CB Radio for Christians," or a complete Fritz the Cat board game, you know the exhilaration of the thrift score. In past issues of **THRIFT SCORE**, *editor Al Hoff has quizzed readers on the weirdest things ever thrifted ("It's a Purse! It's a Phone! It's a Purse that is a Phone!"), collected woeful "the fish that got away" stories ("I can't believe I thought $6 was too much"), warned of safety defects in seventies clothing, and compiled lists such as the one below (with apologies to John Waters for ripping off his style).* Thrift SCORE *teaches an important lesson: Just because something gets tossed aside doesn't mean it's junk, only that it needs to be loved again. Goes for people, too.*

Arrgh! The alarm goes off at 7:45 a.m. You gotta be at the thrifts early. [1] I grab half a cup of joe. I need two cups but thrift stores never have bathrooms. [2] Okay, let's go!

The First Thrift

It's freezing in here and I left my jacket in the car. [3] The thrift is set up so everybody has to sidle down one narrow aisle to reach the rest of the store. [4] It's the shoe and dishware aisle, so it's clogged. [5] There's some guy taking up the whole aisle while he's super slowly moving plates one at a time from one pile to another. [6] Excuse me, excuse me, excuse me—I bug outta there for another aisle. I eyeball a magnificent fold-up snack tray with pink-and-rhinestone poodles watching fifties TV, but it's too awkward to haul around. [7] I hide it between some bad paintings and cut myself on a rusty picture frame nail. [8] Back by the furniture, there is a puddle of water collecting from a drip in the ceiling. [9] An old man is asleep [10] in a cluster of brown plaid sofas. [11] The TVs are on and the sound from the sports show [12] is just a bit louder than the sound from the cartoons [13], but both are still lower than the radio next to them. [14] A man is complaining loudly [15] to a store worker about a TV he bought ten years ago. [16] Oh! A Snow White jigsaw from the forties, the box is in great shape, the pieces look healthy, and it's only 66 cents—66 cents scrawled in black grease marker across the front of the box. Sigh. [17] A super-duper chenille bedspread with huge pink and blue flowers is before me! It's in great shape (and priced low) but weighs a ton and the store doesn't have carts. [18] I turn it inside out on the hanger—it'll be safe that way. I make a mental note to come back and get it. A woman forces a copy of

The Pelican Brief in my face. [19] "Is this good?" she asks. "It's excellent," I lie, and she puts it back on the shelf. [20] I see the guy from a scary collectible shop, retroRETRO, walking out the door with the poodle TV tray. [21] I make a few scores—some books, some curtains. It's time for check out. "This is unmarked"—the clerk throws the curtains behind the counter. It *is* marked, I insist, you just missed the tag. (This is true.) "We don't sell things that aren't marked." [22] The paperbacks are priced according to their original price. I have a stack of fifteen books. The sales lady takes care to caress and turn over each book several times before locating the price, which she then painfully squints at. [23] People in line glare at me. [24] Valuable thrifting time ticks by. [25]

The Second Thrift

It's totally hot in here and now I have to carry my jacket around, since I brought it with me from the car. [26] There's a huge industrial fan in the corner with a sign that says "Not For Sale." [27] It's not turned on. [28] All the shopping carts are taken. [29] The Saturday-Morning-Looking-For-Office-Cubicle-Clothes-Hoggin'-Up-the-Whole-Aisle-People are here. [30] I turn just as some instrument-of-the-devil grabs a photo album full of photos (which I collect!) [31] I pretend to be interested in the adjacent plastic flower pot display. [32] I wait and watch, wasting my time. [33] This stupid person then calls over her stupid best friend and they spend hours going through the pictures, laughing. [34] "Put it back put it back put it back," I mindbeam. They take it. [35] Cruisin' down the coat rack petting the fur coats and checkin' for cool leather. All the leather coats—even the Wilson House of (barely) Leather [36]—are marked way up! Uh oh—sudden shift in values! [37] Some trendy lookin' wannabe [38] is following me and touching everything I'm touching. [39] Yikes, I can't get out of this aisle—there's a shopping cart turned sideways [40] and a generously proportioned lady stripped down to her underpants [41] on the other side. Of course, there's no dressing room. [42] There's the most . . . um . . . "natural" . . . smell . . . [43] Yaaah! She's makin' eye contact! [44] I crawl under a rack of clothes to the next aisle. I knock down some sweaters which are made of that acrylic that makes your fingernails sting [45] and they won't stay back on the hanger. [46] I have dirt all over my legs now. [47] I'm checking out the books. An old guy turns to me and says eagerly "Ancient Egyptians worshipped cats as gods." [48] The books here have price stickers on the front, so when you score a cool pulp, you can't get the sticker off without tearing the cover. [49] I have too many books anyway. I spot the most fabulous little fifties dressing-up-for-lunch suit. On closer inspection, the skirt doesn't match the jacket. [50] I take the jacket—it's cheap enough. I spot a beautiful silk scarf, with half a dozen staples piercing it. [51] Beside me, a shopper is singing "woo-oo-oo, Lipton Girl, woo-oo-oo." [52] I find a delightful woman's sixties parka . . . in the men's coats. [53] Someone runs into my ankle with a shopping cart. [54] The following-me wannabe is touching my parka. [55] At the checkout, after freezing out some bitch that tried to cut in front of me, [56] I hand over my goodies. The clerk rings up the jacket and says, "This is from a suit." "The skirt didn't match." "It's a suit. I can't sell this as a separate piece." [57] I have to collect my things and leave the line. [58] I go to retrieve the evil skirt. [59] I get back in line, which is now twice as long. [60] There is a child grizzling loudly behind me. [61] Louder, louder, louder and now!—full blown hollering. [62] The parent is resolving this situation by ignoring the child. [63] I give a big hairy eyeball to both parties. This gets results. The parent starts yelling [64] at the kid who now starts crying hysterically. [65] I pay, I leave. I've scored some stuff, but man, it's been a rough morning. On my way home, I remember the chenille bedspread. [66]

The Limits of Cheap

Larry Roth created **LIVING CHEAP NEWS** *because he felt the penny pinching tips offered by the standard bearer* Tightwad Gazette *were too complicated. "Most of my friends were members of two-income families," he says. "While we wanted to save money, spending a lot of time at it made for a false economy." This editor's note is taken from a 1994 issue.*

Since launching this newsletter, I've learned different people have different standards of what is truly cheap and what is merely amateur cheap. I want to explore the limits of cheap. One of my readers who uses a one-cubic-foot refrigerator, a hot plate, and lives without a car in a tiny apartment tells me I am not really cheap because I have a 17-cubic-foot refrigerator, a stove, a microwave, a car, and a four-bedroom townhouse.

Another reader in West Virginia is homeless by choice because he doesn't believe in paying for a place to live. I have read about one man who jacks his old Volkswagen off the ground at night to save wear and tear on the tires and another who times his bowel movements so they only happen while he is at work (saving him toilet paper—and no, the article did not say what he does on weekends).

These people have made the choice to live on the fringes of frugality. Their choice does not affect anyone else, and, while they are far more frugal than I am, I applaud their efforts.

But every once in a while I hear from people I cannot applaud. In fact, I often feel like washing my hands after reading their letters. These are people who are cheap at the expense of others. Some don't tip in restaurants because of some "principle," hurting waiters and waitresses. If people do not believe in tipping, they should not eat out. Others make toll calls when they know people are not home, leave a message on the victim's answering machine, and then take advantage of the return call. One woman, upset at having to send a dollar and a stamp for a sample copy of *Living Cheap News*, informed me she was a "true tightwad" and, as a true tightwad, it was her duty to get as many things as possible without paying for them.

If anyone believes I support this perverted noblesse oblige, let's set the record straight. I believe in a "win-win" approach to life. Taking advantage of everybody and everything is win-lose. In the long run, as these people accumulate "free" things that take up space and complicate their lives, their "win-lose" approach will leave them empty. For example, I recently won a fairly expensive prize from a store in my neighborhood that I couldn't use. It was free, so I took it. Eventually I found someone who could use it, but it took some effort to get this "prize" out of my life. Even free things are not bargains if you don't need them.

tools

 Emergency Personal Broadcast TV

This handy device, created by Bill Barker of the mysterious Schwa Corporation, comes from issue 12 of **BOING BOING**.

The Many Moods of the Smiley Face

In 1992, Sam Pratt typed up a funny anecdote, scribbled **ERSATZ** *at the top and mailed copies to fifty friends. "I felt a bit like a crank," he recalls, "which is sort of what I liked about it." Sam has since devoted issues of his pocket-sized magazine of cheap imitation to everything from soft rock to mass transit to bumper stickers and "logos we love." Smile.*

Most any picture you see in a print ad nowadays has been retouched using Photoshop, one of the more powerful graphics programs on the market. Below we've run the classic smiley-face icon through the computer's paces; for the technically-minded, the names of the corresponding "filters" are below:

1. ripple 2. emboss 3. motion blur 4. extrude 5. diffuse 6. distort
7. crystallize 8. zigzag 9. polar coordinates 10. tiles 11. twirl 12. mosaic

tours

The Best Worst Job I Ever Had

"It's just what it sounds like," says Julee Peezlee of her publication, **MCJOB**. *"A zine by and for people who hate their jobs." Julee got the ball rolling in her first issue by describing her shittiest past employment experiences: maid, cafeteria food server, newspaper deliverer, flower deliverer, T-shirt seller. For issue 2, Al Hoff of* Thrift SCORE *shared her recollections of working as a Washington, D.C., tour guide. At last report, Julee was a photo lab clerk; Al describes herself as "a better writer than housewife."*

"Good morning—I'll be your tour guide at Arlington Cemetery this morning. I'd like to remind you to keep your hands and head inside the bus at all times. Our first scheduled stop will be the Kennedy Gravesite . . ."

Yeah, that's me—I was a tour guide, a spiel-giver, a question-answerer on those goofy zoo-buses that make loops around the historical sites in the nation's capital. Hey, it wasn't just a $4-an-hour, miserable, dead-end job—we were instructed to view ourselves as "ambassadors of Washington, D.C."

It was one of the suckiest jobs I've held, and that includes my short careers in ironing, answering an 800 number for Air Force recruiting, selling floor sample furniture out of a tent in a parking lot, recommending gifts at a department store bridal registry, and checking hats. Yet no other bad job provided me with such an unlimited supply of anecdotes. And even now I bet I'm one of less than five hundred people who knows exactly how high the Washington Monument is—five hundred and fifty-five feet, five and one-eighth inches . . . but sinking slowly.

The Job

I answered a newspaper ad for tour guides, passed the "good personality" interview (evidently the scraggly double-processed peroxide hair I had at the time was not a negative), and was signed up for two weeks of training at $3.25 an hour. Training consisted of driving around the route while the spiel was repeated over and over. At the completion of training, you took a written test and did a real-life spiel. You had earned your name tag.

There were two routes—a sixty-minute loop within Arlington Cemetery and a two-hour Mall and Capitol Hill tour. What sucked about giving tours? First and foremost, any job where you deal with the public sucks. The public is rude, sloppy, smelly, noisy, forever eating and drinking, and astonishingly ignorant. I don't expect people to know who donated the Whistler paintings to the Smithsonian, but asking who *lives* in the Washington Monument? Which building *the President* lives in? And no, every tree in bloom is not a cherry blossom!

People exhibited some of the worst behavior at Arlington Cemetery. Even though I'd spell out clearly that Arlington was still a functioning cemetery and not an amusement park, they'd still hang out the bus window videotaping some poor bastard's funeral.

Other miseries of the job included the D.C. weather (cold and rainy or hot and humid), getting stuck in traffic (not just because you had to keep up the patter, but the guide's seat was a hot lump of metal over the engine where you sucked up engine fumes), and the hours. Arrive at 7:30 A.M., leave at 8 P.M. Weekends and holidays were the busiest days, so everybody worked. Over spring break, Easter, and Cherry Blossom Festival, I clocked in on twenty-seven straight days—spewing out the same factoids hour after hour after hour.

Employees

There were bus drivers and tour spielers. The bus drivers were mostly D.C. firemen or city bus drivers making spare cash. The tour-spielers fell into three groups: 1) recent high school graduates, 2) oddballs who truly loved the tour business, and (3) assorted losers. The assorted losers category included myself, the grandson of a forties movie star, a girl so dyslexic she could barely function, and a man who claimed to have been a friend of Elvis Presley's in Memphis. (When I challenged this, he brought in snapshots of himself and Elvis, proving me wrong. When he wasn't passing out candy, he also shilled for Jesus.)

Bossman

There was no boss—just supervisors who carried walkie-talkies and made probably a dollar more an hour. Discussions were limited to "Hoff! Arlington! Bus 21!" I was well liked among the supervisors because I showed up on time and did whatever they said to do. (While I was there, one tour spieler walked off the bus in mid-tour, never to return.) My spiel skills were good, too.

The Uniform

A blue polyester flared skirt, two poly-cotton shirts (one to wear, one to launder), and a blue windbreaker, all with the tour logo. No substitutions allowed. When I went home on the subway at the end of the day, I lived in fear of people asking me questions.

Job Environment

If you weren't on a bus spieling, you were to remain "on call" in one of two trailers—one was behind some construction at Arlington, the other near the snack bar at the Lincoln Memorial. They were single-room trailers, with a soda machine, candy machine, and fridge. No bathroom. You were allowed to either be on a bus or in the trailer—we were prohibited from sitting outside in the fresh air in case we picked our noses or something and belied our "ambassador" status. There wasn't anything to do but sit with the other losers, smoke, and eat candy bars.

The trailer was a Title VII nightmare. Mostly the guys talked—whether white or black girls gave better head, what was wrong with fags, or how hard someone had partied the night before. Firemen would provide disgusting tales of horrors they'd seen on the job. Some of the workers were unhappy listening to all this, but there was nowhere to go. For excitement the drivers would beat the candy machine and distribute the chips and gum.

Perks

Without question the biggest perk was something that almost no one cared about—information. You learned more than you ever wanted to about Washington, its museums, its monuments, marble used, name of architect, year he died and where buried, name of first ship sunk in World

War I and what distinguished it from the ships that came after, the names of all the Challenger astronauts as well as every flowering plant or tree, and where every Port-a-Potty was. (The downside of this is that for years after I quit the job, no friend or relative could come to town without me being enlisted to "give the tour.")

At Arlington Cemetery, employees could collect a key to use a locked stall in the public restroom. This kept you from waiting in line with all the tourists but did not stop them from asking you questions while you were trying to pee.

With your uniform on, in your off-hours, you were free to take the bus tour as many times as you wished (seating permitted). At the end of the day, this might mean a free ride to a subway stop on the route, but you had to listen to someone's spiel. It was strongly recommended that in our spare time (!) we ride around on the buses with the Fanatic Spielers (eight years and counting). Arrrgghhh.

Don't Tell a Soul

Our status as "ambassadors" was strictly governed and this included what we could and could not say on tour during our spiels. This restriction fascinated me and I often tried to work around it. Your presentation was supposed to be free of partisan politics, scandal, or unpleasantness. You were not to use the term "soldier" (which might offend Navy vets); the term "serviceman" was preferred. It was the "Korean Conflict" and the "Vietnam Conflict." (I held my tongue when people asked directions to the "Vietnamese Memorial," as tempting a lead-in as that was!) The Civil War was only to be spoken of in the most general terms and we were to take care to present the Confederate side in favorable terms—D.C. is below the Mason-Dixon line.

My favorite restriction was to never use the phrase "coming up on your right/left" (as in "coming up on your left will be the Lincoln Memorial") in Arlington Cemetery. It was feared that some tourist might think that a corpse was coming up from the grave! "Coming up on your right, the Father of the Nuclear Navy, Admiral Rickover—now a crazed, flesh-eating ZOMBIE!"

I'm all for the First Amendment, but even more so, I'm for interesting tours. It used to frustrate me that I couldn't point out scandalous points of interest: the Tidal Basin where Congressman Mills got caught skinny-dipping with the stripper, the hotel where the Watergate break-in was orchestrated, the "eternal" flame at JFK's gravesite that goes out in the rain.

The End

By all means, visit the nation's capital—but don't call me! Take the tour like everybody else, make it interesting by asking lots of awkward questions, and please, keep your hands and head inside the bus at all times.

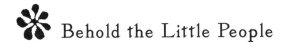

Behold the Little People

Jeff Hansen's **X MAGAZINE** *(now* Dryer Systems*) is chock full of interviews with the likes of Pop Will Eat Itself, the Trash Can Sinatras, and the Inspiral Carpets. There's also stuff like "a day at the demolition derby," reviews of Japanese candy, how margarine works, planning a post-nuclear holocaust road trip (including turning your car into a quickie bomb shelter) and an exhaustive collection of cultural macros ("All <x>, all the time," "Again with the <x>!," "I got your <x> right here!"). In these selections from issue 7, Jeff and Mike McCauley examine the end of an era: the death of the Little People.*

The Little People™ have created some indelible childhood memories. But their legacy came to a grinding halt in 1991, when production of the toys and playsets ended. Fisher-Price bailed on their extensive play family and ushered in a new set of totally redesigned Little People.

How did the Little People maintain such a tight grip on play value? Maybe it was the shapes. Hasbro's Weebles and Playskool's unnamed family set were woefully lacking, being based on eggs and squares, respectively.

Dad started out bald, made of wood. In 1974, he started metamorphosing into plastic, first his head, then his body. Somewhere in the recent past, he acquired a horrible Ted Koppel-like hairpiece that plants him firmly in the seventies.

Mom was typically blue, with yellow hair in a bob. Why wasn't she ever a pilot or a racecar driver?

Boy, a shortened Dad, recently started sporting the hair helmet. Boy was introduced with the Farm, wearing a cowboy hat.

Girl dates to the Goldilocks pull-toy; she later pulled skycap duty at the Airport. She slowly lost her pigtails and now sports a retro-Dorothy Hamill haircut.

Lil' Bullie, the evil twin of Boy, was introduced as the "cranker" for the Ferris Wheel and Merry-Go-Round, and he and his pissed-off carnival worker expression could not be removed from the sets. Over the years, his baseball cap brim migrated from the side to the front of his head.

Lucky, my favorite character, was introduced with the Big School Bus and started out with plastic ears riveted onto its wood head. Lucky was a strange figure in the Little People realm, for two reasons: (1) Another dog that had arms and legs was included with the Farm, a striking parallel to the Goofy-Pluto phenomenon. (2) Having the same basic peg body shape as the other people, Lucky could easily drive a car. —*J.H.*

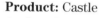

Little People, Little Noise

The Little People all wore smiles. They all lived in wonderful places. Remember the Castle? The Lil' Parking Ramp and its elevator where the floor would tilt toward the ramp and send the family car speeding out of control into the busy streets below? What detail! What fun! And what noise! Every playset had its own sound. They were fine for a few days, but over the weeks they stressed the souls of all parents who heard them . . .

Product: Castle
Action: Dropping person through trap door
Noise: Assorted <clunks> as person banks off walls

Product: Castle
Action: Flicking the flag
Noise: <Binga winga winga>

Product: Schoolhouse
Action: Ringing the bell
Noise: <Ding>

Product: Regular House
Action: Ringing the doorbell
Noise: <Ding>

Product: A-Frame House
Action: Ringing the doorbell
Noise: <tinkle tinkle>

Product: Farmhouse
Action: Opening the door
Noise: <Moooooo> .

Product: Parking Ramp
Action: Attempting to crush person with elevator
Noise: <CLICK CLICK CLICK>

Product: Village
Action: Flicking the streetlight
Noise: <Bunga wunga wunga> (see Castle flag, above)

Product: Village
Action: Sounding the siren
Noise: <eeeeEerrRrrRrRRRERRRAA>*

Product: Boat
Action: Shooting person off diving board
Noise: <Boinga . . . thud> as Lil' projectile lands in next room

Product: Airplane
Action: Throwing plane to see if it can fly
Noise: <CRASH> (Little People fall out)

Product: Family Camper
Action: Push it, push it real good.
Noise: <click click click click click click click click click click>

(The last straw that snaps Mom's mind.)
—*M.M.*

* The bulk of my youth was spent turning that crank, warning the Little People about atomic first strikes and Godzilla.

travel

Eleven Ways to Annoy the Person
Next to You on the Bus

In this "list-o-rama" from the zine **15 MINUTES**, *Kyria Crowley suggests some ways to liven up your next trip across town.*

(1) Ask their name. When they answer, say, "Wow! That's my name, too!" Fifteen minutes later, ask them again. Say "Oh, yeah . . . that's right!" Repeat.

(2) When first sitting down, sink into the seat, breathe a heavy sigh, and exclaim "Ahhhh . . . it's good to be home!" Take out a remote control and pretend to change channels. Say that the batteries must be dead. Fall asleep and snore loudly. Wake up and say, "Hey! I was watching that!"

(3) Place bets on events that have already taken place. Say things like, "I'll lay two to one odds the South wins this Civil War thing."

(4) Spray the seat with Lysol before you sit down. Place a hanky on the armrest separating the two seats. Sit as far away from the person as possible.

(5) Narrate the entire trip. "She walked to the seat, and, eyeing him strangely, decided that this looked like as good a place as any to spend the lengthy trip. 'Hello' she said, but the strange man did not answer, at least, not right away. . . ."

(6) Remark, "Isn't it ironic how the people that you kill are the same people that you need to come to pick you up when you're finally set free?"

(7) Take out a pack of gum and say, "Boy, my ears are popping already!" Talk about how people do look like ants from way up here. Wonder out loud where the stewardess is.

(8) Ask permission for everything you do, like "Mind if I uncross my legs?" and "I was thinking of stretching my arm. Is that okay with you?"

(9) Talk about how excited you are to be on a bus. Sing songs with the word "bus" in the lyrics ("Bus, bus, magic bus") while wiggling around in your seat. Squeal a lot. Take pictures.

(10) Interview the person. Say things like, "Do we have a clip of that?," and "We'll be right back after these messages."

(11) Hang a fishing pole out the window.

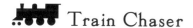 Train Chaser

While assembling the transportation issue of **NANCY'S MAGAZINE** *in 1989, Nancy Bonnell-Kangas asked a colleague, Mark Reinhart, to write about his high-speed hobby.*

I chase trains. Show me a moving train, and I'll climb into my car and chase it. The reason I chase trains is because I feel the only thing more wonderful than having a train speed past me is having a train speed past me repeatedly, and the only way to accomplish this is to keep getting ahead of it. After a train passes, I jump into my car and drive at speeds far exceeding the legal limit to beat it to the next crossing. The thing I like best is to find a stretch of road that runs next to the railroad tracks, and then drive alongside the locomotives for as long as the road stays close. I've chased trains for hundreds of miles at a time.

Normally, you can't just chase trains for hours without some preparation. You need a timetable that tells you the train's departure time and place, stops it will make along the way, and its destination. Also, county maps showing rail lines are a big help. Once you take care of these things, you should invite some friends. Having extra eyes to watch for the train (and the road) can contribute greatly to the enjoyment and survival chances of your trip. Many of my friends have gone train chasing with me and remained my friends.

A friend who is a good photographer can be an asset on any train-chasing trip. He or she can take pictures while you keep your mind on the action. For some reason, train lovers can never have enough train pictures. For example, my favorite engine is the Norfolk and Western Number 611, a streamlined steam locomotive built in 1950. I've chased the 611 around thirty times. My friends and I have photographed the train from every conceivable angle throughout four states—daytime shots, nighttime shots, moving shots, sitting-still shots. I still don't have enough.

You may not believe me, but there are tens of thousands of people who chase trains. There is an even greater number who come out along the track to watch these special steam engines go by. I envy people who can be satisfied just by having the train pass them once. They're happy when the engineer waves to them as the train thunders past. I need the engineer to recognize my face.

ZINE VOICES

"Does the world really need another grubby little zine? Standard answer: None's ever been grubby in quite this way before."
—John Marr, in the first issue of *Murder Can Be Fun*

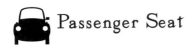 Passenger Seat

*Maria Goodman, editor of **DON'T SAY UH-OH!**, is a great person to ride with cause she'll give you a zine to read. The name of her zine comes from being a passenger as a kid. Her dad was a nervous driver and would caution the young 'uns, "Don't say uh-oh!"*

Passenger Seat

<u>Good People to Ride in Cars With:</u>
1. People who let you turn to whatever radio station you want and don't get mad if you sing along or pause on strange foreign stations with exotic music.
2. People who say "Time to stop at 7-11 and get Zingers and slurpees."
3. People who say "Here, you steer while I take my coat off."
4. People who wave at little kids and honk at perfect strangers.
5. People who say "Hey, let's see where this road goes."
6. People with big old cars with big backseats you can lay in while they drive.
7. People who let you write things in the dust on the side of their car.
8. People who always have enough change on the floor to scrape together enough for some french fries.

<u>Bad People to Ride in Cars With:</u>
1. People who leave up those air fresheners service stations hang on the rear view mirror that smell like stale candy.
2. People who spazz out if you draw pictures in the steam on the window: "That's gonna leave a MARK."
3. People who have power everything and act superior when you can't figure out how to roll down the window.
4. People who instantly turn on the air conditioning when it's the slightest bit warm or sunny.
5. People who won't turn on the heat in the winter. "It wastes energy."
6. People who get mad when you ask if you can change the station; "I've got five decent stations programmed in. Hit one of those."
7. People who spazz out if you stop on a country station for one second just to see if it's this one song you like.
8. People who only listen to tapes and none of them are any good: "Put in 'Party Mix 1987' again."
9. People who make you ask directions, put in gas, and buy food "Because I'm driving."

Things You Never Want to See in Popeye's Arm

It's not about cows, and it's certainly not about juice, although the toy surprise inside makes **MOO JUICE** thick enough to squeeze. Besides his clever cartoons, editor Britton Walters has a hilarious running conversation with a "high school hoodlum"—his younger brother Andrew. For one recent issue, Britton interviewed the creator of the fetish zine Balloon Animals; food editor Heather Ann Baniak explained salami twists; and a sheepish reader volunteered a "slightly edited tale of irony": After discovering his car wasn't actually locked just as the locksmith arrived, he decided to avoid an embarrassing moment. As you can imagine, it didn't work out.

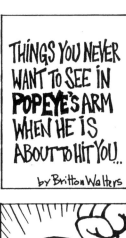

The Brutality of
"Little House on the Prairie"

When Lisa Carver says she publishes **ROLLERDERBY** *because "it's a good excuse for dates with the interviewees," she's only half-kidding. She met her partner, provocateur Boyd Rice, after sitting him down for a Q&A published in her thirteenth issue (they've since split). This examination of "Little House on the Prairie" is typical of the interview/conversations you'll find within, along with gems like a quiz comparing the mutterings of Tiny Tim and Vladimir Zhirinovsky, a rundown of famous epileptics, and an interview with the Singing Flea Market Cowboy.*

"Little House on the Prairie," says Shaun Partridge, is the unsung hero of TV shows. Widely believed to be a mediocre, dorky family show, it is actually the most violent, dramatic family show of all time. Like "Little House," Shaun's appearance is unthreatening. Twenty-six, blond/blue, he is a weird person who commits petty crimes and tricks on strangers and acquaintances, often hurting people's feelings. He doesn't care as long as he has fun. He has always been polite to me, but I'm watching him.

Lisa: What did that guy do to make Pa's friend squeeze him so hard blood came out?

Shaun: I don't remember. I only remember the charm of it. It was chunky red hemorrhage blood.

Lisa: I remember what led up to the fight: Pa hocked his violin so he could get a hat for Mary's birthday, then Ma found out and sold the hat and got the violin and Mary told Pa that the best gift he could give her was to play his violin. I can't remember how that led to Pa's friend squeezing the blood out of someone—but you know how things just happen in the Wild West.

Shaun: That's what I liked about "Little House"—it was honestly brutal. As a kid, I always felt cheated by TV. The violence was so fake. "Little House" was real. People died horrible deaths. My absolute favorite episode was when Albert met a girl, fell in love, then she got raped. I fell in love with the girl. It was intense—her strict, evil father would make her cinch her breasts because they were too big. He said boys have wandering eyes. He'd drag her home and say [through clenched teeth], "Cinch it! Cinch it!" It was creepy. There was this evil blacksmith with a sick clown face—a porcelain harlequin mask with painted-on red lips. No one knew him, but it was like he had always been there. He would watch Albert and the girl when they held hands and kissed. One time Albert went home and the blacksmith raped the girl in the woods. She ran away to an old barn. Albert would bring her food. The blacksmith came to rape her again and Albert went berserk and whacked him with a pitchfork. The girl fell or was pushed off the loft and died. Her last words were, "I'll always love you, Albert." He said, "I love you, too." He was crying.

Lisa: What made you fall in love with the girl?

Shaun: She was just real soft. Another good episode was when the citified grandson comes to live with his grandparents.

Lisa: Yes, and he threw the old man down the stairs.

Shaun: The old man said, "That didn't happen, Ma. He didn't mean it—it was a mistake. I roused him too early."

Lisa: Then he throws the old woman down the stairs!

Shaun: Yeah! No, he didn't throw her down.

Lisa: I know, Shaun. I was just trying to excite you.

Shaun: Oh! Ha, ha!

Lisa: Did you see the beginning of that episode, when it shows why the grandson got so mean?

Shaun: No.

Lisa: It started with his dad complaining about supper, and his mother is doing everything to avoid getting hit, and then the kid walks in and says, "Hi Dad." The dad says, "You ripped your shirt!" There was a little tear in the kid's shirt. The dad says, "I buy you shirts and you rip 'em? Here, let me show you how you really rip a shirt!" And he rips it to shreds while it's still on the boy's skinny little body, then he throws the kid against the wall and says, "I'm sick of this place—you people really irritate me." So he runs out and goes drinking, and that's how he gets killed—he does the same thing to a grown man and the man shoots him.

When the kid grows up and steals Pa's watch, Pa gives him a choice of working for him or going to jail. Pa knows the guy was abused, but the guy still has to suffer the consequences of his actions like everybody else. And when the guy refused to do the work, he thought Pa wouldn't do anything because he was the grandson of Pa's friend. But Pa put that bad boy in jail! That's what I liked about Pa—he didn't mess around.

Shaun: Yeah. It was disturbing, though, how in any tense situation they had to call him "sir." "Any of you kids seen my watch?" "No, sir." I never cottoned to that.

Lisa: You're a guy, so you see that authority as a threat. I'm a girl, so I see it as, "Oh my, Pa's taking care of everything." I'll say "sir" to him! You're worried that Pa will lock you in jail! He should, some of the things you do.

Shaun: I appreciate the strictness now, but I hated it when I was a kid. Remember the hospital? There were a lot of weird things going on in the hospital.

Lisa: What hospital?

Shaun: The hospital. It was small and made out of logs, but it was a hospital.

Lisa: You mean Doc's house?

Shaun: Yeah, I guess it was Doc's house. People were always ashen and feverish and gangrenous.

Lisa: And kids were always falling off horses and faking comas in order to wreak revenge on someone. Except Laura—she's so tough, when she fell off her horse, the horse died. Did you see the one where Nellie faked being paralyzed and Laura shoved her down a hill in her wheelchair? Nellie fell face first in a swamp and her mother saw and almost had a heart attack and died.

Shaun: That was intense. Another classic episode is when Albert smokes a cigar and burns down the house and kills Mary's kids. They had to go to the funeral. He killed his sister's kids.

Lisa: It's funny how they keep repeating themes. I can think of two barn-burning episodes. One was a kid lit off a firecracker in the barn. Another was a kid burned down a barn with a lantern and it was blamed on the town racist, and the black guy on the jury was the only one who voted not guilty.

Shaun: There was a racist on "Little House"?

Lisa: Yeah, that old man who lived on the outskirts of town.

Shaun: Back then in real life everyone was racist.

Lisa: In the Little House books, Pa's idea of a fun time was to organize a minstrel show. What did you think of Mr. Oleson?

Shaun: He's definitely a sissy boy.

Lisa: He was a good man, he was just weak. With the right woman he would have been strong, but in those days you were stuck with whoever you married. He wasn't tricky enough to make the situation work for him, and he wasn't strong enough to fight his way out of it. He was truly a tragic character.

Shaun: Ha, ha, ha!

Lisa: What, you don't think he was tragic?

Shaun: Totally. When he went cheating I felt so happy for him—the woman was nice to him, he had so much fun, he felt so young. They were dancing around the parlor.

Lisa: He had an affair? That's shocking.

Shaun: She was city folk. She was Irish. She turned out to be a whore—he walked in on her kissing another man, her brother or something.

Lisa: He was kind of handsome except he had that look in his eyes.

Shaun: That worn and beaten look.

Lisa: He coveted Laura as a symbol of goodness. I think it was Kierkegaard who said comparison is the source of all unhappiness. He was always comparing his entire family to Laura.

Shaun: His daughter Nellie disturbed me.

Lisa: She looked kind of normal, but at the same time it was like she was one step away from being deformed.

Shaun: Mary looked weird, too.

Lisa: She looked like an alien.

Shaun: I didn't like Laura either.

Lisa: I thought you would—she's such a prankster.

Shaun: I've never liked redheads.

Lisa: Are you this hard to please in real life?

Shaun: No. The thing is, I like strange skull structures, but certain ones are disturbing.

Lisa: How did you feel about Pa and Ma's work ethic?

Shaun: I hated it! Working so hard they'd *pass out!* I think it's unhealthy to wake up before you want to. It's completely cruel.

Jaina Davis, a rich girl growing up in a decadent environment, was spellbound by the poverty and strict morality of the Ingalls family. But what's really shocking is that her favorite character was the vindictive, gossipy, obnoxious, rich, racist, mean old shrew Mrs. Oleson! Jaina is twenty-five years old.

Lisa: I can't believe you love Mrs. Oleson!

Jaina: I love the whole Oleson family. They reminded me of an insane version of my family. Nellie was a spoiled snooty brat and I always emulated her. My favorite episode was when Nellie invited all the rich girls to a fancy birthday party, and she invited Laura too to make her jealous. So Laura invited all the town girls out to her "country" party. She led all the girls in their beautiful party clothes to the river bank. Mary, the good girl, removes her shoes and very daintily walks along the edge of the water, picking up her skirt, being careful not to let it touch the dewy grass. Laura, bad girl, leaps into the river and convinces all the other girls to go in, too. Then Laura points out a "special place" to Nellie where it's the warmest and most pleasant spot to stand. Nellie stands there a long time, very smug. Then she runs screeching out of the water—she has leeches all over her legs!

Lisa: That was great. And you're supposed to burn leeches off, but Laura told Nellie and her friends that you pull them off—actually that just makes the leeches hold on tighter and when you do pull them off blood spurts out. The girls were running screaming through the woods, ripping their dresses on the branches, blood streaming down their legs, crying and filthy. Laura was laughing so hard!

Jaina: Mary looked at her like, "You're so immature. I'm telling Ma." Mary was so damn proud of herself. She was *so, so, so* sorry that she went blind, but she had the *courage* to go on staying in her family's house and playing the organ for the rest of her life. I can't stand her! She always made Laura feel guilty for having a good time.

Lisa: She followed every rule exactly.

Jaina [hateful voice]**:** And she was blind but she could crochet *lace.* Remember when Mary was trying to pretend she was getting her sight back? Stupid bitch. I hate her. I remem-

---

ZINE VOICES

"Creating something that transcends capitalism (i.e., losing money hand-over-fist) is a revolutionary act. That's why I don't care too much for zines trying to get bigger and bigger. If they succeed, all they've achieved is creating another consumer good."

—Alphonse Coleman, *Bubba's Live Bait*

ber the music swelling as she walked over to the window and looked up toward the sun with hope in her eyes and it turned out she just felt the heat, she wasn't seeing any light.

Lisa: They had her cry every episode cause she's such a good crier.

Jaina: And her stupid blind husband—why do both of them have piercing blue eyes? They're blind so all of a sudden their eyes get really bright?

Lisa: Do you remember when blackbirds came by the thousands and ate all the crops? Pa shot 'em. So they lost the crops, but they had blackbird pie all winter. Ma fried them in their own fat. Can you imagine living during those times? I'd say, "I'm tired of blackbird pie." Ma would say, "This is all your food for the day." All those people living in two rooms . . .

Jaina: Did Ma and Pa have sex in the same room as the kids?

Lisa: Can you imagine Nels and Harriet Oleson doing it?

Jaina: I imagine her in rubber.

ZINE VOICES

"As I write this I am on a production deadline for *Pawholes* #6 and have been deprived of sleep, nutrition, and rational thought for seventy-two hours. I adore this wigged-out feeling and the crunch of the very end: the mucusy crud of rubber cement on my fingers, the White-Out vapors seeping into my precious lung tissue, the floor a sea of scrap paper and paste-ups gone awry."

—Deborah Barkun, *Pawholes*

Wind Tunnel? Sure!

In 1993, Jeff "Keffo" Kelly was temping at an insurance company. Fed up after being strung along with the promise of a permanent job, he produced a zine called Welcome to the World of Insurance: An Intro to Corporate Hell *and handed it out to the full-timers. That led to the bitterly funny* **TEMP SLAVE!**. *"I can't draw for shit," Jeff explains, "so I rearrange what I see in mainstream publications instead. I'm interested in producing belly laughs and helping people see beyond the facade of corporate bullshit." This selection appeared in the third issue.*

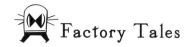 Factory Tales

It's easy to be creative in art school. But once you drop out and find yourself inspecting air conditioning units, it takes more resolve. While working at factory jobs during the summer of 1994, Tyler Starr entertained himself by sketching his surroundings and jotting down stories from co-workers. "My pockets were filled with these drawings and notes, so I started **THE BUCK IN THE FIELD***," he says. Tyler's sketches and ear for dialogue capture the frustrations of doing work that many Americans forget needs to be done. "You reach the point of no return," one delivery driver told Tyler. "I figure I was stupid enough to stay this long, it would be stupid to leave."*

Our Chief Field Researcher ,Tyler "Where's My Wallet" Starr, shown here trying to leave suburbia in his transportation *The Buck.* Note his factory gear, $0.75 safety glasses and a headband composed of a yellow sponge and a large rubber band, both of which were purchased from the Temp company. He keeps a job until he learns where the fire exits are located.

Resume
Jobs Tyler Still Remembers

Locale	Job Research	Nickname
Vernon, CT	Dishwasher	Hey
Warehouse Pt, CT	Prison Shelf Builder	Hate You Temps
Fishkill, NY	Spotlight Hanger	Buddy
Enfield, CT	Car Battery Stacker	
Providence, RI	Hospital Transporter	Little Buddy
Mansfield, OH	A/C Muffler Maker	Wildman
Columbus, OH	Cinnamon Barrel Scraper/ Cappuccino Syrup Bottler	Old Buddy
Galion, OH	Salt Water Taffy Maker For State Fairs	Buddy
Manchester, CT	EMT	Manson
Springfield, MA	Passion Fruit Bottler	Pal
Hartford, CT	Cardboard Box Stacker	T

Gary and I were eventually left unsupervised in a warehouse where we were supposed to scrape the bottom of cinnamon barrels eight hours a night. I have included the layout of the place in order to show our pallet-jack racing route as well as some of the other notable sites.

a   Candy machine (yielded 2 packs of licorice when turned upside down)

b   Private office blocked with pallets (Temps had stolen a pen from here)

c   Bathroom with broken door (Gary hit it with pallet-jack)

After Hours at the *Sports and Sudz*

1A Carl: bottler. on the job conversation- "Boy, somebody must really want this stuff"

2A Carl's Wife: an assembler. we only observed her holding Carl's beer

3B Edna: secretary. "my first day at work for the medical office they showed me an x-ray of a penis. It hardly fit on the screen"

4B Merle: forklift certified. when asked about his interstate Golf trips "we don't do so well, we're all beer drinkers"

5A S. Shaky: bartender

6A Sonny: died this year after falling off the scaffolding while trying to build a bar with his partners, "a round for Sonny!" "another one for Sonny!"- the bar owner wanted his ashes so he could put them up with the whiskey bottles

6B unknown

7A Booker: assembler. he had four girlfriends at a time. His wife claimed their son was in jail and they needed money to bail him out. Edna went to her sock drawer and gave it to them. Booker later turned up in Texas.

Pathetic Doug: Babysitter

An ex-girlfriend once told Doug Holland: "You've got no money, no friends, you live in a slum, you never do anything interesting, and you're too damn fat to have sex. Your life is pathetic." Little did she know she would be naming a zine. Doug launched **PATHETIC LIFE** *in 1994 and has since filled more than twenty issues with details of his ordinary but piquant existence. "I've been told I'm too pessimistic," he says. "Well, I live in the real world. This society stinks, the government is evil, and all religion is a sham, and anyone who says he's satisfied with life is a liar. Other than that I'm downright chipper." Three months after this entry was written, Andrea and her daughter Shannon moved to Philadelphia to live with Andrea's new fiancé.*

Shannon was giggling at my silliness, but I didn't go to the
kitchen, of course. My job was to keep an eye on her, and from
the kitchen I wouldn't have been able to see if she started playing with matches or explosives or otherwise needed overseeing. I
sprawled across the sofa, put plugs in my ear to drown out the
television, and read zines for a while. She talked during the
commercials, mostly about school, but otherwise she wasn't much
bother. When the tv started to really get on my nerves, I said,
"Any chance you'll turn that damn trash off? Wanna play chess or
checkers or hangman or something?"

"We're not allowed to swear in this house," she said, but not
all snotty. It sounded like she didn't much care, like it was
just another rule. She thought hangman would be more fun than
tv, so while she got a tablet to write on I quizzed her about the
no-cussin' rule.

"I don't want to get either of us in trouble," I explained,
"so can you tell me which words I'm not allowed to say here?"

"Well, I'd have' to say 'em."

"Yeah, but if you don't tell me which words I can't say, I
might say all the wrong words, just accidentally. We've got no
rules at my house, so I'm used to saying whatever I damn well
please."

"You're not supposed to say that," she said, giving me a long
looking over, deciding once and for all whether I was to be
trusted. "You're not supposed to say damn, fuck, shit, and
piss," she said, and started laughing.

"Damn, fuck, shit, and piss," I repeated. "Got it. I'm not
gonna say damn, fuck, shit or piss all night."

"Or asshole."

"Right," I waved my finger. "No damn, fuck, shit, piss or
assholes. If you think of any other words we shouldn't say, be
sure and let me know." And I'll be damned if she didn't think of
several others.

Guess she was obnoxious as hell, but I didn't give any orders
so she had no way to disobey, and we got along fine. She was
very knowledgeable and talkative about her mother's sex life,
too. Seems Mom doesn't have any romance, and often complains
about not having a man around since the divorce. Tonight, she
said, was her mother's first date in months. I feigned interest,
just to be polite.

She also talked about some kid at school who's been bothering
her. Sounds like he's got a crush on her, but doesn't know quite
how to express it, so he keeps slugging her arm. Giving her the

benefit of my grown-up wisdom, I told her she'll meet lots of men in life who'll want to express their affection by slugging her, but if she lets them they'll just slug her again and again. I also suggested she tell the teacher, but she said the teacher's "a dickwad."

When she got tired of playing hangman, I let her read a few of my zines. She particularly liked THRIFT SCORE and DISHWASHER, and since I'd already read them I said they were hers.

For dinner we baked a frozen pizza that was awful, but she scarfed down most of it. When her bedtime came, 9:00, she said, "aw," and that was protest enough for me. I hated bedtime when I was a kid, so I said I sure as shit -- oops -- wouldn't enforce the rule now. Besides, seeing as I'd promised I wouldn't touch her, what could I do? We watched TERMINATOR 2 on the vcr till she fell asleep, at about 11:30. I put the tape away and washed dishes, hoping to make a good impression with Andrea, and maybe be invited back for something better than babysitting.

Heard a car door slam at about half past midnight, a few foot-steps later came a key in the lock, and Andrea stepped in. We chatted for a minute -- her date went badly, the guy was a lout -- and then she roused Shannon from the easy chair.

"Hi, honey," she said. "You ought to be in bed."

The kid came wide awake quicker than you'd expect, and said, "Oh Mom, Doug was the coolest babysitter."

"Why, thank you," I said, flattered and surprised to hear it. "And Shannon was perfectly behaved as well. In fact, I wish I could hug her good night, but of course that would be improper." And she bolted from her mom, ran to me, and hugged my big belly. After joking about it off and on through the evening, that was actually the first time we'd touched since shaking hands hello.

As Mom nudged the kid out of the room, I noticed that the hangman sheets were visible under the zines, with S H I T H E A D rather obvious on top, so I hurriedly picked up the pages while Andrea's back was turned, folded 'em tiny and slipped them into my pocket.

After she'd tucked Shannon into bed, Andrea and I talked for a couple of minutes. Mostly about me, damn it, when I'd rather have talked about her. Then she paid me (I doubt her regular sitter makes $30 a night), and I tactfully implied that more reasonable rates could be negotiated for next time. I had the distinct honor of unzipping her dress, before she thanked me and shooed me out, closing and locking the door.

As I walked to the bus stop, it started to rain again.

Neglected Topics

*Enamored with Melvil Dewey's library book classification system, Nancy Bonnell-Kangas once assigned a Dewey decimal number to each article in her zine, **NANCY'S MAGAZINE**. This selection, written by Nancy (a librarian herself), was given 370.19.*

CHEMISTRY
Chapt. 24: NUCLEIC ACIDS
  A. The Genetic Code
  B. Genetic Mutation &
      Genetic Disease
  c. Viruses ← a ha

MUSIC: An Appreciation
Section 40: Koto Music of Japan

The Problem of Philosophy
chapter 18: The Value of Philosophy

S O C I O L O G Y
20. SOCIAL CHANGE, SOCIAL MOVE-
    MENTS, & COLLECTIVE BE-
    HAVIOR
  A. The Consequences of Change
    • The Domino Effect

SOCIOLODY
XII. Social Change & Technology
  A. Modernization & World Systems

Sociology
Part 7: WAR & PEACE
  Prospects for Peace
    1. Disarmament
    2. Collective Action

Orienation to the Theatre
5: The Audience
    Opportunities for the Audience

Clerical Office Procedures
Section 10: You & the Office

ANIMAL SCIENCE
XXIII. Horses
  • Selecting & Judging Horses
  • Feeding & Managing Horses

Sometimes it's out and out loss of ambition. Sometimes it's snow days. Sometimes it's an unusually intriguing middle section.
Whatever the reason, the fact remains. No teacher ever makes it to the end of the textbook.
We at N's M began to wonder about the effect this may be having on humanity. Could this phenomenon account for critical gaps in knowledge?
The last chapter in Botany is entitled, "Anglosperms." We've never heard of anglosperms. See what we mean???
Our research teams scoured textbook tables of contents and came back with shocking results. Shown here is a selection of final chapters and their final subheadings for your comparison to the current world situation.

TENNIS
Part 9: Playing the game
  • Where can you play?

BADMITTON
Chapter 20: The Laws of Badmitton
  A. The Language of Badmitton

Main Problems in American History
XX. Reconstruction: The Nation's Un-
    Finished Business
  • The Return of White Supremacy

Interpretations of Amer-ican History
Chapter 89: The Reconstructive Era:
    Constructive or Deconstructive?

AMERICA: PAST & PRESENT
    from 1865 to now
Section 11: The Reagon Era
  • Reagon & the World

GEOGRAPY: Regions & Con-cepts
XXX. Southeast Asia: Between the
    Giants
XXXI. Antarctica

The Writer's Way
chapter 74: Essay Tests

BASIC ENGLISH REVIEW
Chapter 99: Word Choice
  A. Like and As
  B. As-as, As-so
  c. Between and among

370.19
Educational sociology

How to Order a Zine

1. Send well-wrapped cash for best karma.
2. Allow a few weeks for delivery; they got jobs.
3. Write and tell 'em what you think.

Basura (Basurame)
P.O. Box 33
Boulder, CO 80306
three bucks (checks: Bob Bellerue)

Batteries Not Included
130 W. Limestone St
Yellow Springs, OH 45387
three bucks (checks: Dick Freeman)

Beer Frame
160 St. John's Pl
Brooklyn, NY 11217
three bucks (checks: Paul Lukas)

Ben Is Dead
P.O. Box 3166
Hollywood, CA 90028
five bucks (checks: Ben Is Dead)

bOING bOING
11288 Ventura Blvd, #818
Studio City, CA 91604
five bucks (checks: bOING bOING)

Bubba's Live Bait
P.O. Box 824
Knoxville, TN 37901
one buck and two stamps (cash only)

The Buck in the Field
55 Horizon Circle
South Windsor, CT 06074
one buck (cash only)

Bust
P.O. Box 319
Ansonia Station
New York, NY 10023
three bucks (cash only)

Chip's Closet Cleaner
P.O. Box 11967
Chicago, IL 60611
three bucks (checks: Chip Rowe)

Chum
P.O. Box 148390
Chicago, IL 60614
three bucks (checks: Dan Kelly)

Cometbus
P.O. Box 4279
Berkeley, CA 94704
$2.50 (cash only)

Crank
P.O. Box 633
Prince Street Station
New York, NY 10012
three bucks (checks: Jeff Koyen)

Crap Hound
P.O. Box 40373
Portland, OR 97240
five bucks (checks: Sean Tejaratchi)

Crimewave U.S.A.
P.O. Box 980301
Ypsilanti, MI 48198
three bucks (checks: Mark Maynard)

Don't Say Uh-Oh!
P.O. Box 5871
Kansas City, MO 64171
one buck and two stamps (cash only)

The Duplex Planet
P.O. Box 1230
Saratoga Springs, NY 12866
$2.50 (checks: David Greenberger)

ecdysis
2457 W. Cullom, #2
Chicago, IL 60618
two bucks (cash only)

8-Track Mind
P.O. Box 90
East Detroit, MI 48021
two bucks (cash only)

Ersatz
441 W. 37th St, 2nd floor
New York, NY 10018
two bucks (cash only)

Farm Pulp
217 NW 70th St
Seattle, WA 98117
three bucks (checks: Gregory Hischak)

FAT!SO?
P.O. Box 423464
San Francisco, CA 94142
$3.50 (checks: Marilyn Wann)

15 Minutes
P.O. Box 49497
Austin, TX 78765
one buck (cash only)

Flatter!
P.O. Box 40608
San Francisco, CA 94140
four bucks (checks: Jaina Davis)

funkapotamus
P.O. Box 63207
St. Louis, MO 63163
one buck and two stamps
Flying Saucer Attack: five bucks
(checks: Jerome Gaynor)

Heinous
P.O. Box 10412
Portland, OR 97296
two bucks (cash only)

Hey! Hey! Buffet!
1200-A Crestwood Rd
Austin, TX 78722
one buck (cash only)

Hitch
P.O. Box 23621
Oklahoma City, OK 73123
four bucks (checks: Rod Lott)

Inquisitor
P.O. Box 132
New York, NY 10024
five bucks (checks: Daniel Drennan)

It's a Wonderful Lifestyle
P.O. Box 515
Brisbane, CA 94005
four bucks (checks: Candi Strecker)

Kooks
P.O. Box 86663
Portland, OR 97286
five bucks (checks: Donna Kossy)

The Last Prom
120 South San Fernando Blvd, #243
Burbank, CA 91502
three bucks (checks: Ralph Coon)

Living Cheap News
7232 Belleview Ave
Kansas City, MO 64114
one buck and one stamp (cash only)

McJob
P.O. Box 11794
Berkeley, CA 94712
two bucks (cash only)

Meanwhile . . .
America Online
keyword "Meanwhile"

Milkcrate Digest
P.O. Box 1412
Providence, RI 02901
one buck and two stamps (cash only)

Mommy and I Are One
P.O. Box 643
Allston, MA 02134
three bucks (checks: Jessica Hundley)

MOO juice
P.O. Box 11619
Chicago, IL 60611
three bucks (checks: Britton Walters)

Murder Can Be Fun
P.O. Box 640111
San Francisco, CA 94164
two bucks (cash only)

Mystery Date
P.O. Box 641592
San Francisco, CA 94164
one buck and two stamps (cash only)

Nancy's Magazine
P.O. Box 02108
Columbus, OH 43202
four bucks (checks: Nancy's Magazine)

Pathetic Life
537 Jones St, #2386
San Francisco, CA 94102
three bucks (cash only)

Pawholes
P.O. Box 81202
Pittsburgh, PA 15217
four bucks (checks: Deborah Barkun)

Pills-a-Go-Go
1202 E. Pike St, #849
Seattle, WA 98122
two bucks (cash only)

Preparation X
P.O. Box 33561
Raleigh, NC 27636
two bucks (cash only)

The Realist
Box 1230
Venice, CA 90294
two bucks (cash only)

Reign of Toads
P.O. Box 40498
Albuquerque, NM 87196
five bucks (checks: Reign of Toads)

Roctober
1507 E. 53rd. St., #617
Chicago, IL 60615
three bucks (checks: Jake Austen)

Rollerderby
P.O. Box 474
Dover, NH 03821
three bucks (checks: Lisa Carver)

The Secret Handsignals of the DBA
P.O. Box 7205
Minneapolis, MN 55407
one buck for catalog (cash only)

Shark Fear, Shark Awareness
1420 NW Gilman Blvd, #2400
Issaquah, WA 98027
three bucks (checks: Darin Johnson)

Sidewalk Bubblegum
P.O. Box 245
Capitola, CA 95010
one buck and two stamps (cash only)

Sidney Suppey's Quarterly &
Confused Pet Monthly
P.O. Box 515
Brisbane, CA 94005
two bucks (checks: Candi Strecker)

Stay Free!
341 Lafayette St, #558
New York, NY 10012
three bucks (checks: Carrie McLaren)

Teenage Gang Debs
P.O. Box 1754
Bethesda, MD 20827
three bucks (checks: Erin Smith)

Temp Slave!
P.O. Box 8284
Madison, WI 53708
three bucks (checks: Jeff Kelly)

Thrift SCORE
P.O. Box 90282
Pittsburgh, PA 15224
one buck and one stamp (cash only)

TV Grind
559 W. Surf St, #805
Chicago, IL 60657
three bucks (checks: Dean Williams)

Underbelly
1004 Franklin Place
Rockford, IL 61103
two bucks (cash only)

Verbivore
532 La Guardia Place, #573
New York, NY 10012
three bucks (checks: Jeremy Braddock)

View From the Ledge
P.O. Box 8306
St. Petersburg, FL 33738
one buck (cash only)

Voices From Spirit Magazine
P.O. Box 4301
Portland, ME 04101
two bucks (cash only)

X Magazine (Dryer Systems)
P.O. Box 1077
Royal Oak, MI 48068
three bucks (checks: Jeff Hansen)

XYY
82 Kimball Ave
Yonkers, NY 10704
four bucks (checks: John F. Kelly)

Zines About Zines

Factsheet Five
P.O. Box 170099
San Francisco, CA 94117
six bucks (checks: Factsheet Five)

Obscure Publications
45 S. Albert St, #1
St. Paul, MN 55105
one buck (cash only)

Zine World
924 Valencia St, #203
San Francisco, CA 94110
three bucks (cash only)

Zine Catalogs

Atomic Books
1018 N. Charles St
Baltimore, MD 21201
three bucks

Mind Over Matter
1710 Central Ave SE
Albuquerque, NM 87106
two stamps

Primordial Soup Kitchen
P.O. Box 1312
Claremont, CA 91711
one stamp

Qvimby's Qveer Store
1328 N. Damen Ave
Chicago, IL 60622
three bucks

Reading Frenzy
921 SW Oak St
Portland, OR 97205
one buck

See Hear
59 East 7th St
New York, NY 10003
three bucks
Store: 33 St. Marks Place

For a free guide to starting your own zine, send a self-addressed, stamped envelope to The Book of Zines, P.O. Box 11967, Chicago, IL 60611, or E-mail zinebook@hholt.com.

index